Goin' Up Home

Goin' Up Home
premiered in June 2022
in The MeX (Martin Experimental Theatre),
Kentucky Center for the Arts,
Louisville, Kentucky.

Script by **Scout Larken Link**
Directed by **Gilmer McCormick**
Original Score & Sound Design by **Stephen Reinhardt**
Produced by **Susan McNeese Lynch**
for **Eve Theatre Company**

&

... original cast ...

EMILY	**Karole Spangler**
LIZ	**Meg Caudill**
HALLIE	**Liz McFerron**
ANNIE	**Ellie Archer**
TESS	**Susan Crocker**
FURMAN	**Sean Childress**
GARY	**Eric Sharp**
LOLLY	**Michelle Chalmers**

... crew ...

STAGE MANAGER	**Brandi Hornbuckle**
SET DESIGN	**Kathryn Spivey**
LIGHTING DESIGN	**Nick Dent**
COSTUMES	**Sharon Harrah**
BOARD OP & PROPS	**Ashley Nicole Sims**
PROPS	**Cindy Carroll**

GOIN' UP HOME

A Play in Two Acts by

Scout Larken Link

GOIN' UP HOME
A PLAY IN TWO ACTS

Scout Larken Link

FICTION

ISBN 978-1-934894-74-3

*

*This script is dedicated to Liz Fentress, Gilmer McCormick,
Susan McNeese Lynch & Stephen Reinhardt,
who nurture and inspire joy through mentoring & collaboration.
Also, in honor of my rural family, with gratitude.* -SL

*

COVER IMAGES BY JEN THEODORE (FRONT) & MONA EENDRA (BACK) - *UNSPLASH*

Goin' Up Home was initially conceived and drafted as part of the Kentucky Voices
playwriting project at Horse Cave Theatre. It was subsequently developed and
expanded with funding assistance from The Kentucky Foundation for Women.

PUBLISHED IN KENTUCKY BY

Motes
Books
DRAMAWORKS

& AN AMPERSAND PROJECT &

PRINTED & BOUND IN THE UNITED STATES OF AMERICA

INTRODUCTION

NOTES FROM THE PLAYWRIGHT

A NOTE ON LANGUAGE:

This play is set in rural Kentucky. It is important that readers or actors who have not lived in rural Kentucky refrain from assuming exaggerated brogues or accents when imagining or speaking the words of these characters. Artificial speech (the kind too often witnessed in inaccurate regional portrayals on television and in movies) is almost never true to these folks— nor is any such superficial mimicry true to any rural or ethnic peoples. Regional speech in rural America is not an affect, nor should it be judged or performed in that way.

Every cultural group and regional locale has some innate speech patterns that could be deemed "quirky" to outsiders, and the "Southern accent" varies wildly from region to region, state to state. More specifically, speaking styles vary notice-ably from one end of Kentucky to the other, especially near the borders it shares with any of the seven states surrounding it. Seven neighbors—north, south, east and west! Native Ken-tucky dialects are influenced by locations as diverse as Illinois and Tennessee, or Virginia and Missouri. If you had to desig-nate one state as the obvious "hub" of the eastern half of our nation, Kentucky just might be it. Get out your map (or open your app) and have a look. We're kind of a crossroads of interactions moving in many directions, rich in neighbors, roads and rivers. Lots of folks from lots of places. Lots of "accents." Notably, folks living in west Kentucky speak in some ways dif-ferently from folks living in the state's Appalachian mountains. Likewise, folks living in south central Kentucky (not that far from Nashville, Tennessee) differ from those in northern Kentucky (sometimes referred to as "Cincinnati south").

Bluntly put, the rural South in general is no more valid a target for linguistic ridicule or caricature than is Manhattan or Maine or Manitoba or Madagascar or Martinique. Just allow the characters to speak in their own unforced manner. It's what they say that matters, after all.

A NOTE ON SPECIFICITY OF PLACE:

I grew up a stone's throw from the confluence of the Mississippi and Ohio rivers on *"the west coast of Kentucky."* (Yes, I'm the writer who originally coined that phrase.) That's where **Goin' Up Home** takes place. Geographically, this region is different from most of the rest of the state. Lowest in elevation, for one thing. I've heard it called Kentucky's Delta, draining the many rivers and creeks running downhill from the mountains to the bluegrass to this four-rivers region—officially known as The Jackson Purchase (the other two rivers are the Cumberland and the Tennessee, which both empty into the Ohio, which empties into the Mississippi.)

The Jackson Purchase is the Commonwealth's "add-on" region. It wasn't part of the original Virginia territory, from which Kentucky was formed in 1792. The Purchase was annexed by state government legislation in 1818 after purchasing it from the Chickasaw Nation. This eight-county region had long been a seasonal hunting ground for the Chickasaw people. And centuries prior to that, it was settled by "pre-historic" (weird term, that) civilizations that we now call mound-builders.

But that was then. Things have changed, people have changed, but the rivers are a constant feature.

Having lived in many places, both urban and rural, in and out of the Commonwealth, I attest to the fact that people—and in particular, rural-roots people—are much the same everywhere. That said, be assured that rural folks, *politically* at least, are *not* the same as each other ... at all. The "broad brush" pundits are so thoroughly wrong in this regard. You might be surprised how many progressive activists and liberal voters are rural!

Now, there are notable differences between the generic "western" Kentucky (being pretty much everything west of Louisville) and <u>west</u> Kentucky (being only the Jackson Purchase region and, perhaps, the westernmost counties of the Pennyrile—those that border Lake Barkley and the Cumberland River). To me, western Kentucky is "west-ish" while west Kentucky is "true west" (some folks say "far west"). Unless you're from this place, you probably don't make that distinction: west vs. western. But I am, and so I do. And though variations do exist from region to region, Appalachian writer Belinda Mason put it best when she wrote, "It's still Kentucky, all the way to the Mississippi River!"

The Purchase has been home to Governors, U.S. Senators and a Vice-President. The oldest and most famous annual political event in the state happens there. Again, we know politics. From birth. Admittedly though, the political changes I have witnessed since my childhood there have been alarming.

There are fine writers who have hailed from west Kentucky too, but most are not as well-known as those from other parts of the state. However, I'm delighted to say that one of our past Kentucky Poets Laureate lived right there in the very tiny hamlet nearest my family's farms where I grew up. Post office, couple of churches, teeny grocery ... and a Poet Laureate! As a child, I knew him; his wife was a teacher of mine.

Much later, another writer native to that region became a bestselling novelist whose book was adapted to film. Yet another was a famous humorist in the early 20th century whose stories also became movies. Others have written interesting histories and historical novels about the place.

For that matter, my own grandmother was a published poet and essayist. My grandfather, my uncle and I represent three generations of editors, publishers and journalists. My high school best friend founded and publishes the largest magazine in that entire region. Our home area has spawned novelists, historians, medical writers, poets, journalists, screenwriters, playwrights, songwriters, sci fi scribes, essayists, textbook authors, columnists—you name it.

So, whether you've heard or not, we've got literary chops. Admittedly, our tales are often more about rivers and cropland and small-town county seats than about mountains or metropolises. Those other places can best tell their stories, and we can best tell our own. We tell them to each other all the time anyway, generation after generation.

A NOTE ON PROCESS:

Telling this story has been a journey. I wrote the first draft of this script (it was initially a one-act) in 2006 while participating in the brilliant Liz Fentress's playwriting classes through the Kentucky Voices project at Horse Cave Theatre, but some of the stories this play comprises had been knocking around in my head for decades. A play turned out to be the literary form that best suited how to present these particular yarns—alongside the many fictional bits and pieces that flesh out the action in *Goin' Up Home.*

Since its inception, the script has undergone many revisions, as is the way with writers and writing. Kentucky Foundation for Women provided generous support during one segment of that period. That's when it grew from one act to two.

Workshopping *Goin' Up Home* through collaborations with an amazing pair of theatre, film & TV professionals, Gilmer McCormick & Stephen Reinhardt, brought the script home in ways I wouldn't have gotten to on my own.

All these people and organizations provided exactly what I needed at exactly the right times. I'm forever grateful for their support, ideas, experience, genius and utter brilliance.

Being immersed in rich storytelling traditions (on both sides of my family) went a long way toward my development and intuition as a writer. For one thing, it taught me something about empathy. For another, it gave me an ear for the nuances of language ... and of intention. Words can be weapons, but words can also be tools. (I like the notion that swords actually *can* be converted into plowshares, as I learned in our tiny Methodist church's Sunday School all those long years ago.)

For decades, I've practiced (and taught other writers) this truth: *In the specific we find the universal.* The stories I heard growing up, while specific to the places and people of my own origin, translate to universal human experiences—as do all good stories well told. After all, the human experience applies to us all. Minute specificity of detail provides context, but the broader human experience applies to us all. Human living is wrapped up in urgency and ugliness, pleasure and leisure, grief and greed. We adore, we ignore, we despise, we refuse, we accept, we regret, we avoid, we embrace— we address our challenges with courage, or else we lurk in the shadows of our cowardice. In all ways, humans persevere. We manage living somehow. At least for a time.

A NOTE ON FAMILY STORIES:

Now, let me be very clear: When it comes to ***Goin' Up Home*** in particular, some of this story is grounded in "truth" (whatever that even means anymore)—meaning that fictionalized versions of my family stories weave in and out of it)—while much of it is wholly imagined. (For example, these characters are not directly based on my real relatives, friends or acquaintances.)

Importantly, some of this story is *yours*, too, if it's alive in your mind. (I revere all the ways in which audiences and readers interact with my work, as should be the duty of all serious writers.)

But make no mistake: *All* of ***Goin' Up Home*** is real. That's because all of it is human.

May this specific story do its universal duty in reminding you of your own memories, allowing you to "hear" lost voices, inspiring you to remember what shocks and delights you ... and, most of all, providing you thought-provoking enjoyment in a universal story about specific people and places that you may or may not already know.

By story's end, perhaps you'll feel that you do indeed know them. And that's what universality can do, for it's what our shared human experience—at its best and at its worst—is all about.

So, here's your homework: Tell your family stories to the young people in your biological or chosen clan. Repeatedly. They may not seem to care much about them now, but in years to come when they think of you and of the tales and personal history you shared, they will treasure what you gave them. And they will know themselves just a little bit better, too.

—*Scout*

CHARACTERS

EMILY – 50s-60s; the slightly older of a pair of
double-first-cousins; grounded & nurturing

LIZ – 50s-60s; slightly younger of the two cousins;
at times edgy; harbors emotional pain

HALLIE – 18/40; Emily's niece; Liz's first cousin once
removed;
as young HALLIE, age 18, she's naïve &
youthfully jaded, yet whip smart;
as FUTURE HALLIE at 40 (*Prologue* & *Epilogue*),
she's the mature keeper of the family's stories

FURMAN – 70s; bearded; Emily and Liz's uncle;
brother of Gary & Lolly; a rock of the
family; rides a Harley

GARY – 70s; Liz's father/Emily's uncle; brother of
Furman & Lolly; family troublemaker

LOLLY – 60s; Furman & Gary's 'baby' sister;
Emily & Liz's aunt; artistic & eccentric

ANNIE – 20s-30s; visibly pregnant young mother
from long-dead generation; sister to Tess;
lived in same farmhouse around 1900;
grounded but grieving

TESS – 20s-30s; sister to Annie; from long-dead
generation; lived in same farmhouse around
1900; guilt-ridden

SETTING

All action takes place inside and outside a farmhouse in rural west Kentucky, late springtime. Scenes occur both during the *present* time and as flashbacks to *circa 1900*. Characters are costumed according to their respective eras. Lighting will also indicate the shifts between present day and flashbacks.

Two set areas are required: one interior room (kitchen); one exterior space (wide back porch and yard).

Because the *present day* farmhouse has been unoccupied for a number of years, the kitchen is relatively empty, and tall grasses have grown at corners of the porch. The place, however, has not been completely ignored and, therefore, is not in derelict condition.

During all *flashback* scenes, an electric light bulb hanging in the window is replaced with a coal-oil (kerosene) lantern, and the porch/kitchen are altered with props to indicate that the house is well-kept and occupied.

FAMILY TREE: characters referenced & implied in *GOIN' UP HOME*

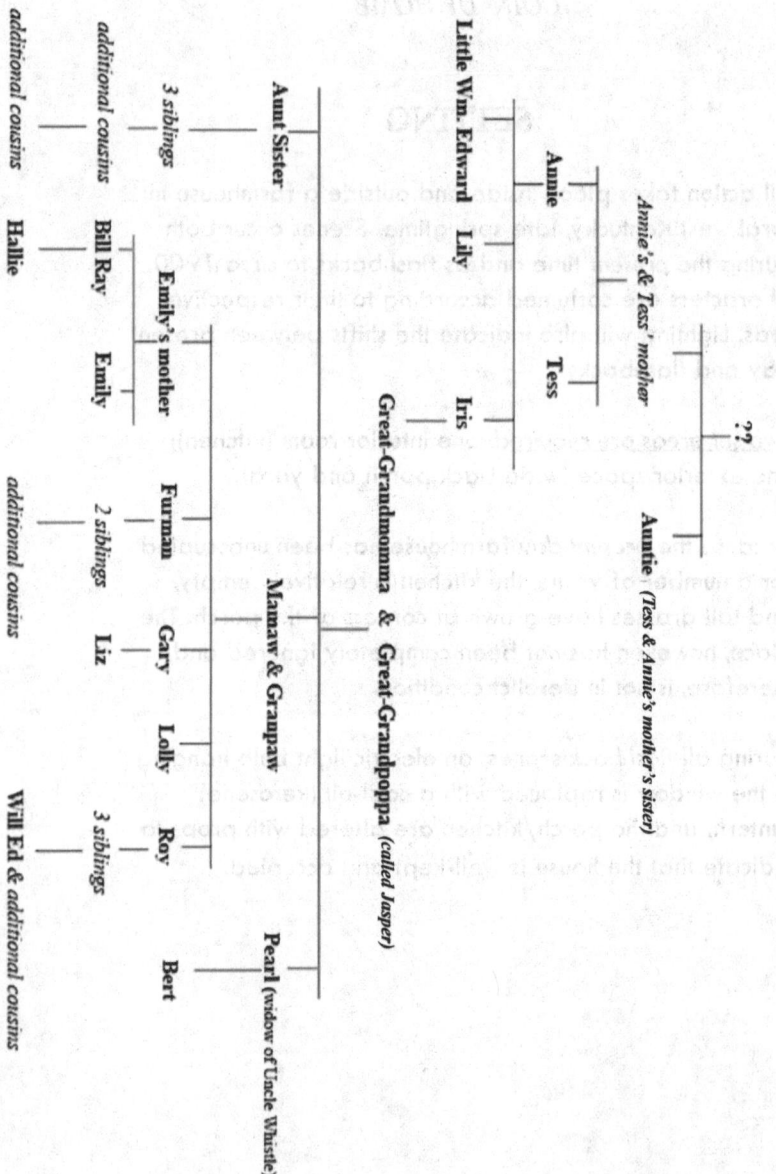

Little Wm. Edward Lily

Annie's & Tess' mother

Annie

Tess

Iris

??

Auntie *(Tess & Annie's mother's sister)*

Aunt Sister

3 siblings

additional cousins

additional cousins

Bill Ray

Hallie

Emily's mother

Emily

Great-Grandmomma & Great-Grandpoppa *(called Jasper)*

Furman

2 siblings

Gary

Liz

Lolly

Mamaw & Grampaw

Roy

3 siblings

Bert

Pearl *(widow of Uncle Whistle)*

Will Ed & additional cousins

ACT I

PROLOGUE

[Lights rise on 'FUTURE HALLIE.' (At age 40, she is separated in time from her relatives.) She is downstage right in isolated light, standing at a small table, unpacking and perusing items from an old pasteboard box (the same box and items we will see her discover as young HALLIE in Act I, Scene 7). She handles photos, a letter edged in black, two coins, and a <u>skeleton key</u> on a necklace chain, which she admires lovingly, then places around her neck. As she works, she softly <u>hums</u> and finally <u>sings</u> two lines of the hymn "FARTHER ALONG" (traditional/public domain)*.]*

FUTURE HALLIE. Farther along we'll know all about it
              Farther along we'll understand why

[Lights fade as she sings the last line, leaving HALLIE in darkness. She exits with the box of items.]

SCENE 1

[At rise, scene is <u>outside</u> farmhouse in the river bottom and bluff lands of west Kentucky, near the confluence of the Mississippi and Ohio rivers, <u>circa 1900</u>. <u>Late afternoon</u>. Unroofed back porch; open double windows; a wooden screen door leads into a kitchen. The place is well-kept. The porch holds functional objects indicating everyday life, including a farm dinner bell mounted on a post. Characters are dressed in period clothing.]

[ANNIE, (circa 1900) a visibly pregnant woman in her 20s or 30s, opens the screen door and stands holding it open. She wears an apron over her dress.]

ANNIE. *[shouts]* Tess? Tesssssie!

[ANNIE enters onto the porch. As the door slams behind her, a

skeleton key falls to the porch floor. She picks it up, shakes her head, and replaces it on top of the exterior doorframe. She crosses to the dinner bell and rings it three times.]

ANNIE. *[shouts toward offstage]* Hallo-o, Te-ess! Willie?!

[ANNIE then appears to see them offstage in the distance. She waves her arm over her head in broadly, smiling.]

ANNIE. *[shouts]* Supper's on the table!! Y'all come on up t'the house and wash up!

[She gives the bell one last peal, waves again, wipes her hands on her apron and exits into the house.]
[Lights fade.]

SCENE 2

[Lights up. Scene is at <u>outside</u> same farmhouse. <u>Springtime</u>. <u>The</u> <u>present</u>. <u>Dusk</u>. The place is vacant, but not debilitated, indicating that though it's now unoccupied, it hasn't been completely ignored. Well-worn back porch with open double windows (screened) and a screen door leading into a kitchen. A few clumps of tall grasses stand at the corners of the porch. The dinner bell remains on its post. A naked light bulb hangs lit inside the open window.]

[EMILY, a woman in her 50s or 60s, is sitting at the picnic table, gazing at the sunset, listening to the radio. A partially-eaten piece of pie on a saucer sits on the table. There is a mop bucket near her; a rag mop leans against the porch wall. She is dressed in 'housework' clothes, a dish towel drapes her shoulder.]

[LIZ, a woman of roughly the same age (EMILY's double-first-cousin), dressed in 'housework' clothes and wearing an apron, enters the porch, backing through the screen door, a saucer of pie in one hand and a broom in the other, and is a bit surprised to find EMILY already there.]

LIZ. *[leaning broom against porch wall, surprised]* Well. What in the world you doing out here, cousin? Finished up already?
EMILY. What're <u>you</u> doing?

14

LIZ. I asked you first.

EMILY. Just did the last of the parlor. Mamaw always kept it so nice. I want everybody to feel like home when the rest of them get here.

LIZ. I'm missing her more now than I ever have, I think, Em. She sure did love this place. She'd just die if she knew.

EMILY. If she wasn't already dead.

[They share a familiar, ironic giggle, tinged with a bit of shame for it.]

LIZ. It's been a day, hadn't it, Em? You found the Spic & Span?

EMILY. [nods and indicates the bucket.] You okay?

LIZ. [slightly irritated] No, Emily, I'm not. Whatever would give you the impression that I might be? I'm only losing my whole ....

EMILY. [consoling her cousin] I know it's hard. For me, too. For all of us.

LIZ. Of course. Of course I know that. But now I'm losing the very last of her ... and maybe the best of me. [a beat] I can't fathom how we're going to get through this, is all. I may have to bail out on you.

EMILY. Oh, no you don't! You'll make it, Liz. You will. We'll do it together, every step of the way.

LIZ. It's just ... Emily, it's too much ... too many loose ends or something. [groans, then desperately attempts a subject change.] Look, you want some pie?

EMILY. [picks up pie saucer] Got some. I'm surprised you found it, though, what with old Bert hiding it in the least likely places.

LIZ. Well, it wasn't easy. You remember how he used to hide Aunt Sister's fried pies.

EMILY. Oh, my heart! Those peach ones she made that were s'good. I'd give a hundred-dollar-bill right now if I could go back in time and get her to teach me how to make those things. Lord, they were something.

[A beat as they each reminisce.]

LIZ. I put the bedspread on in the back bedroom.

EMILY. Which one?

LIZ. The one with the hand-embroidered edges. It looks good on that old iron bedstead.

EMILY. I always loved that one. Wonder what'll happen to it?

LIZ. Please, don't let's talk about it. Please.

[*They eat in silence for a beat.*]

EMILY. Seems like she started with dried fruit ... cooked in sugar. And rolled out homemade crust.

LIZ. Huh?

EMILY. Aunt Sister. Fried pies. She'd make up a big huge batch of 'em, and she'd have 'em all laid out to cool on the biggest cake plate she owned ...

LIZ. ... and then old Bert would come in and catch everybody gone and eat about a half dozen.

EMILY. And then he'd take and put the plate – for later on—way up in the good-dishes cabinet, or on top of the Frigidaire, or somewhere nobody'd think to look.

LIZ. He's a fool for anything with sugar in it.

EMILY. Ever'body's got their own weakness, and that's his.

LIZ. But Mamaw loved that nephew of hers. She always defended him like she would one of us. Said his sugar craving was from him being a boy during World War II when sugar was rationed and scarce. I don't know how many of us have called him out on that – hiding food – but it doesn't seem to faze him one little bit. He just grins and goes on about his business as usual.

EMILY. You know how Aunt Sister used to always say, "Come on in this house, honey child – I've just finished baking you a cobbler." ... Or a mess of fried pies, or a German chocolate cake, or whatever she had.

LIZ. She always was baking something ... her excuse to have sweets around.

EMILY. Truth to tell, now. Aunt Sister had her a sweet tooth too.

LIZ. All of us cousins and whoever else might come by – she'd always say, "I know it's your favorite." Make you feel special every time. But when she'd say it to Bert, he always took her so ...

LIZ & EMILY. ... literal.

[*They chuckle.*]

EMILY. Center of the universe.

LIZ. He's got his ways.

EMILY. He's good though.

LIZ. He is.

[*They eat.*]

LIZ. What kind you got?

16

EMILY. Coconut cream. Aunt Pearl's recipe, I think. You?

LIZ. Preacher's wife's pecan.

EMILY. Where'd old Bert hide it this time?

LIZ. Inside that broken warming drawer underneath the old oven.

EMILY. I found this'n in the linen closet.

LIZ. Well, that's a new one.

EMILY. Still-and-all, I'm glad old Bert stopped by. It was good to see him, wadn't it? [*chewing & thinking for a beat or two*]

LIZ. Damn, I hate this. I hate this whole thing.

EMILY. I know.

LIZ. But what you don't know is <u>how much</u> I hate it. How can life have the nerve to just ... go on? [*She eats, thinks, then attempts again to escape her pain by a change of subject.*] Great-Grandpoppa used to hide things too. Kept him a pint of peach brandy, and he'd hide it from Great-Grandmomma.

EMILY. Great-Grandpoppa did that? I never knew him to drink.

LIZ. He didn't, really. He just kept it around for a little nip now and then — and to drive her crazy.

EMILY. Well, you know it would. Her and her self-righteous ways.

LIZ. He did a pretty good job of hiding it, but he'd get a big kick, too, out of watching Great-Grandmomma stew when she'd run up on one of his secret bottles.

EMILY. Moved it around, did he?

LIZ. Some. But mostly he kept it in the toilet tank. When she'd find it, she'd pour it out, all the while raising Cain. He'd sneak and buy him another one and stick it someplace else for a while. After she'd gone and checked the toilet tank again, he'd slip it back in there. She'd forget about watching for it for a while, and then Katy-bar-the-door when she remembered to look again and there it was — bigger'n life and half empty, to boot!

EMILY. I bet he loved that.

LIZ. Oh, he'd laugh ... you know how he was ... laugh 'til tears'd roll down his face. [*another shadow crosses her thoughts*] Did you remember to dig out that pasteboard box from the dormer closet? The one with Uncle Roy's old

17

Lionel set in it?

EMILY. I did it first thing. It's sittin' in there by the pie-
safe.

LIZ. He was pretty specific about it. You 'member how
you and I used to play with that toy train — set up a
figure-eight track around the legs under the dining room
table. How it had that strong electric-burning smell when
you'd plug it in? That little crossing gate that went up and
down and rang a bell? Mamaw said not to tell Roy she
let us play with it — that he wouldn't like it.

EMILY. And him a grown man at the time — off in the
Army. I swear.

LIZ. [remembering defensively] It was just a toy. Kids are
s'posed to play with toys. And anyway, I never meant to
break the little smokestack off the caboose.

EMILY. Don't worry about it.

LIZ. You think he'll be mad, Emmers?

EMILY. He hasn't looked at that old thing since he went
off to the service more'n 40 years ago. My lord, don't
worry about it.

LIZ. I've worried about it for 40 years. Wonder why
people are funny about that stuff?

EMILY. Funny 'ha-ha' or funny 'odd'?

LIZ. Odd.

EMILY. I don't know, but they sure are. You want some
coffee? I'm going in.

LIZ. It'll have to be decaf for me. I can't do all that old
caffeine like I used to.

EMILY. Same as me.

LIZ. I think there's some instant in there someplace. In
that sack I brought in.

EMILY. I've already perked us a pot. I'll get us some.
[exits into house where she is seen through window]

LIZ. [points to sky, raises voice to be heard] Shootin' star!

EMILY. [calling back through the window] Make you a
wish!

LIZ. [to herself or to no one in particular] Don't tell,
though, or it won't come true. [gazes at the stars]

[EMILY enters with coffee cups.]

LIZ. Hey, Emmers, did you ever see one of those great
old big meteor showers?

18

EMILY. Don't reckon.

LIZ. I did. Once. When I was still living out here, just before Mamaw died. Pitch black dark, and all of a sudden, here they come! Sky raining full of 'em – one right after th'other! Like God threw out a pan of dishwater, and all the drops were stars, flying across the sky, all different sizes, all lit up. Then a few stragglers. And then another whole pan of 'em flung across the sky. Oh, I wish you'd seen it, Em. It went on for hours, seemed like. I fell asleep looking out that upstairs window and it still going. I sure made a lot of wishes that night.

EMILY. [smug] I saw a lightning bolt split a tree to smithereens one time.

LIZ. Did you?

EMILY. Right out the kitchen window here.

LIZ. When was this? Where was I?

EMILY. Prob'ly in your bassinet. I wasn't but maybe three myself.

LIZ. How in the world can you remember something from that far back? Lord, I can't remember what we had for supper last night.

EMILY. Somebody – Uncle Whistle or Mamaw or ... who was it? – was holding me, in front of that window over the sink [points to the window]. There was a gang of us in there; BIG storm going on – hail and lightning popping all around. Wasn't a whole lot of <u>rain</u>, though, as I recall. Does that seem odd to you?

LIZ. Did it scare you?

EMILY. I think they thought I was scared, but I wasn't. Didn't know to be. Too little, I reckon. I b'lieve the grownups were holding onto me because <u>they</u> were a little scared of what might be headed our way.

LIZ. Kind of like I'm feeling now. You never were scared of much, Em – I'll say that for you.

EMILY. It came from out of nowhere. Big old bolt. Splintered that mimosa tree in the side yard. All. To. Pieces. Smoke and slivers of wood flew everywhere.

LIZ. [gestures to the yard, empty of mimosa trees] <u>What</u> mimosa tree?

EMILY. Exactly.

LIZ. And you weren't scared?

EMILY. I just remember thinking, 'Well, would you look at that.' I know my eyes had to be big as Ben Franklin half-dollars.

LIZ. It's sure funny what people remember, isn't it?

EMILY. What's one of yours?

LIZ. [a beat or two as she thinks a few seconds] The time I ran off and hid in the top of the corn picker, I guess.

EMILY. In the corn picker?

LIZ. They say I was about three. Maybe four. Big enough to walk ... and climb, I reckon. I don't remember getting up in the thing, though. I just remember being up in it.

EMILY. Were you by yourself?

LIZ. [nods] Entirely. For the first time in my young life. Hey, that's something, isn't it? That I can actually remember the very first time I was independently alone. [A beat. Then wistfully ...] Lord, I felt free.

EMILY. You didn't go off looking for freedom. At the tender age of three?

LIZ. I just wanted to see could I get up that high, I reckon. Or see what things looked like from up there. Or maybe I was just up in the contraption before I realized, I don't know.

EMILY. And they didn't know where you were?

LIZ. Nawsir. And I knew to answer when they called me — I was old enough to know that — but I didn't answer. I just hid up in the top and looked down on Mother and them scrambling all over the barn lot looking for me. They were kinda frantic.

EMILY. Lizzard, you little shit.

LIZ. I know it. I remember I was up in there, and it was just about getting dusky dark. It started gettin' cooler — didn't have anything on my arms, just a little thin t-shirt. Mother was standing up on the slats of that old wooden gate over yonder, leaning over, and calling and calling — calling me out by my name. And I just sat up in there, and watched to see what she'd do next.

EMILY. Who found you?

LIZ. I don't know. I guess either I finally hollered or got too cold, one or th'other, and started climbing down. I don't remember the beginning or the ending — I just remember being up in there, and seeing all of 'em frantic, and feeling like I didn't have to answer right then if I didn't want to. It was probably the first time in my life I made a conscious decision. I didn't like scaring Mother, though. I remember she was pretty shaken up. She said later that she didn't know whether to hug me or spank me when I showed up safe. Said they were getting ready to go drag the pond to look for my little corpse.

[They sit quietly together for a moment, drinking coffee and thinking separate thoughts.]

EMILY. You were lucky you had Mamaw after you lost your mom.

LIZ. I don't know what would have happened to me if it hadn't been for Mamaw. My daddy sure wadn't an option. Never has been.

[A beat.]

EMILY. Saturday's going to be a big day.

LIZ. It'll be a hard day. I never wanted to see it come.

EMILY. But it has to.

LIZ. Does it?

EMILY. You know it does.

LIZ. I still despise it.

EMILY. I keep asking myself, over and over, what is it about this old homeplace that makes me love it so much? Makes it mean s'much to both of us?

LIZ. You know the answer to that one.

EMILY. Mamaw. It's not the place so much as it's _her_. She made it what it was for us.

LIZ. She sure loved that old river out yonder.

EMILY. She loved both those rivers. Snakes and all.

LIZ. *[quoting Mamaw]* 'The Mighty, Muddy Mississip' and…

EMILY & LIZ. … 'The Waters of the Wide Ohio.'

EMILY. I always loved to hear her talk about wanting to put one foot in each river at the same time.

LIZ. She did it, too.

EMILY. She never!

LIZ. Yes ma'am, she did! She'd talked about it all those years, you know, so one day – oh, I don't know, a few years before she died – Bert drove her over to Cairo *[pronounced KAY-ro]* and walked her off the point there at old Fort Defiance.

EMILY. Well, I'll be!

21

LIZ. Yessir! [stands and mimics the event] He helped her wade out in there past that rocky riprap, just shy of those awful old currents and, by god, she planted her right foot in the Mississippi and her left in the Ohio.

EMILY. Wouldn't that have been a sight?!

LIZ. I'd give anything to've seen it. You know her grin had to have been wide as both those rivers put together.

EMILY. 'No second chances,' she always said.

LIZ: We'd all do well to learn that lesson. [Then she clouds over.] A river'll roll, all right. Just like Time itself.

EMILY. And we cain't do a thing to stop it.

LIZ. It's never the same river twice.

EMILY. I wake up out of a dead sleep in the night some-times — sit bolt upright up in bed in the dark — hearing Mamaw call my name. Plain as day. I swear I do.

LIZ. I believe you.

[They pause, thinking separate thoughts.]

LIZ. Did you throw coal-oil up into that wasp nest we found out on the front porch today? [coal-oil = kerosene]

EMILY. Yep.

LIZ. Kill em all?

EMILY. Ever' last one.

LIZ. Knock it down?

EMILY. Yes'm, Miss Bossy Britches.

[They sit looking at the sky, thinking, resting, waiting together.]

EMILY. [Gestures across the yard] The old chicken coop is fixin' to collapse one a these days.

LIZ. It's a goner. The brooder house, too. Been no chicks out there for a long, long time.

EMILY. It's a shame too, no chickens.

LIZ. Yeah, 'cause I love me some fried chicken dinner. Mmm-Mm-Mm-Mmm.

EMILY. Well, who doesn't?

LIZ. [after a beat.] You want a refill?

EMILY. [taking a last swallow of coffee before handing off her cup] Mm-hm, thanks.

[LIZ crosses toward the house. At the door, she notices a skeleton key lying on the porch floor. She picks it up. She lifts the key high to show EMILY.]

EMILY. [knows the key has a habit of falling.] Again?

LIZ. Some things never change. [*She chuckles, shrugs, returns the key to the top of the door frame, its usual place; then she enters the house.*]

EMILY. [*Calls toward the kitchen window.*] How in the world did they do it in the old days?

LIZ. [*Entering from kitchen.*] Do what now?

EMILY. Do everything! Big old families — and everything used to be so hard before the 'lectric came all the way out here. And automatic washing machines. And automobiles, tractors, party line telephones. I'm talking about 'way back. Just think about it, Lizzie.

LIZ. I know it! I don't know. What about having to put in a garden, and smoking hams, and canning or drying all their food to get through winter? And all without getting the weather forecast a week ahead.

EMILY. You know these people that talk all the time about getting 'out in the country.' The only time you think something is 'out' is when it's somewhere different from the place you are 'in.' You know what I mean?

LIZ. Hmm. Come to think of it, the only time we ever say we live 'out in the country' is if we are talking to someone from town. To us, we're just living in the country.

EMILY. [*Watches LIZ setting the coffee cup on the porch floor*] You know, you've got Mamaw's hands.

LIZ. [*pleased*] You think so? I've always thought maybe so, but I didn't know for sure.

EMILY. You do.

[*LIZ smiles at her hands. There is a thoughtful pause.*]

EMILY. Have you heard from your daddy lately?

[*a beat*]

LIZ. Not since he got out of the pen this last time.

EMILY. Any idea where he might be?

LIZ. I worry he's layin' up drunk somewhere. Or dead in a ditch. I wish I could fix him.

EMILY. It's not your fault. Not any of it. You do know that?

LIZ. I can't seem to ....

EMILY. Your daddy's his own man with his own ways, Liz. Always has been. You miss him, though, don't you?

LIZ. I don't know why, but I do. When he's around, he brings nothing but pain. But when he's not, that hurts my heart, too. [*a beat*] You're really going to make me do

23

this, aren't you?

EMILY. Yep.

LIZ. Even if I decide to do it, I don't have to like it, do I?

EMILY. No, cousin, you most definitely do not have to like it. [a beat] All right, then. C'mon, Suzy Q. Let's get up and go it again.

[They start to collect themselves and the objects near them.]

LIZ. We need to get it done, I reckon.

[EMILY reaches down to grasp and gently squeeze both of LIZ's clasped hands in one of her own, then picks up her cup, stands, and exits into the house.]

[LIZ picks up her coffee cup and follows EMILY into the kitchen.]

[HALLIE, a young woman, age 18 (EMILY's niece / LIZ's younger cousin), enters from across the yard.]

HALLIE. Lizzie Bit! Auntie Em! Y'all here? Anybody home?

EMILY. [calling out window] In here, Hallie! The kitchen!

[HALLIE steps up on the porch and absent-mindedly gives the old dinner bell a single clang, as if she has done it many times before.]

HALLIE. [as LIZ and EMILY enter the porch from kitchen] I should have known I'd find y'all back here with the baked goods and fried foods.

EMILY. Young lady, you mind your manners with your elders, now. We can get mean as snakes if we're provoked.

HALLIE. But nobody lives here anymore. Is everybody in this family just weird? I mean, look at us. Here you two are, out here polishing a deserted old falling-down house for no apparent reason. And you're always telling stories about dead people.

EMILY. Hold tight to stories, Hallie, for they're life's lessons.

HALLIE. Speaking of life lessons, there's some that don't ever learn them. Take Uncle Gary, the family jailbird, for god's sake. I mean, come on, how crazy can you get? And ... [realizing her faux pas, embarrassed] Oh, god, I'm so sorry, Liz. I ....

LIZ. Be back in a minute. [exits into the house]

HALLIE. [groans] What did I just do?

EMILY. It's okay, Hallie. Don't worry too much about it. You didn't mean to. Liz knows that.

24

HALLIE. Crap.

[*LIZ enters with resolve.*]

LIZ. You know what? My dad is a little nuts. A LOT nuts. Nobody knows that better than I do. But that's my life, see? That's what I've got.

EMILY. There's not a soul in this whole family that hasn't got regrets about one thing or another. We stick together. [*pats LIZ's arm*] It helps.

HALLIE. I don't know what I was thinking.

LIZ. Dad's troubles are his own — not yours, not even mine. He's done a lot of things that've hurt us all. You spoke the truth. That's never wrong, kiddo. I'm a little jumpy lately.

EMILY. The point, I think, is that we all have our pride and our shame. Who's to say if one's a blessing or the other's a curse?

LIZ. Comes out different in different people.

HALLIE. Should I be sorry I came by?

LIZ. Oh, don't be silly, Silly. I'll get you a bowl of cobbler.

HALLIE. Are you kidding me?

LIZ. It's nutritious.

EMILY. Sure — it's got fruit in it! And it's so good.

HALLIE. I have to watch my intake. I've got a swim meet next week.

LIZ. Rather have pecan pie? 'Cause nuts are good for you too, you know. Natural.

HALLIE. [*to EMILY*] Will you call off your hound, please?

EMILY. You're just gonna dry up and blow away one of these days, girl.

HALLIE. Don't worry about me.

LIZ. It's our job, dear ... to worry about you.

HALLIE. Well, don't. I don't know why I bother with you two, I really don't. Now can I get a hug from anybody around here?

[*The cousins encircle HALLIE in a group hug.*]

[*Lights fade.*]

SCENE 3

[*Lights come up. Scene is inside same farmhouse kitchen at night, circa 1900. Characters are dressed in period cloth-ing. There are more furnishings in the room; it looks "lived*

25

in." Light bulb no longer hangs in view. Instead, there is a dim light from a lantern hanging in the open kitchen window.]

[ANNIE is removing a large bowl and some cloths from a wooden table. On the table is a body (articulated mannequin) completely covered by a sheet. From the size, it is obvious that this is a child's body; ANNIE has been washing it in preparation for burial. She busies herself in this work, wringing out a rag, moving slowly but steadily in silence about the kitchen, to and from the body, lifting a hand or foot to wash it. She gently smooths or pats the sheet as she works.]

[TESS stands very still outside, as if in semi-trance, virtually unnoticed, watching ANNIE through the window. She neither moves nor speaks. She watches ANNIE and gazes vacantly on the covered corpse. ANNIE finishes her work (she has clearly been attempting to find things to do) and looks around the room, searching for something else, something else — then finally pauses, steps to the corpse and places her hand on the child's covered head. Her grief finally comes forth; sobs shake her. TESS averts her face, drops her head, turns her body slightly away.]
[Lights fade.]

SCENE 4

[Scene is outside the farmhouse, <u>night</u>. <u>The present</u>. The window and curtains are open, and the light bulb hangs in the window. A mop and bucket and a few sacks and boxes sit about on the porch, as well as a large cooler. EMILY and LIZ have been drinking a little bit of bourbon; the bottle and two plastic cups are present.]

[As lights come up, HALLIE is gathering trash bags and moving them. EMILY and LIZ, listening to the radio, are finishing singing along with a song; then they laugh.]

LIZ. [Switches off the radio.] So, Town Girl, how's your momma?
HALLIE. She's fine, I guess. Working too hard, as usual. You'd think that new second-hand store was her whole life.

She's pretty excited about it.

EMILY. And that unruly daddy of yours?

HALLIE. Oh, he's just the same as usual. Full of piss and vinegar.

EMILY. Did you hear that, Lizzie? My brother is brimming with urine and wine gone bad.

LIZ. Same sweet old sourpuss, huh?

HALLIE. Can't get enough of himself. Plays golf all the damn time.

LIZ. Watch your mouth, young lady. Don't you know that's a dirty word?

HALLIE. What? 'Damn?' What are you, six years old?

EMILY. No. 'Golf.' That word offends us modest working-class folk. [gestures to HALLIE] Come sit by me. Tell us what you're doing way out here.

HALLIE. When I heard you two crazies were out here cleaning up this old place, I figured it was time for me to come around and see what's what. So?

LIZ. So ... what?

HALLIE. So, what's what? What're you two up to?

LIZ. Oh, the usual—cleaning house and telling tales.

HALLIE. Tales? What kind of tales?

EMILY. You know, stories of dreams, visions, those strange things passed down to us.

HALLIE. Dreams, huh?

LIZ. Oh, dreams are big in this family. And sometimes they're lessons too.

EMILY. Yeah, we've all got it — us women, anyway — one way or another. Some of us have dreams that we don't know what to do with ...

LIZ. Mamaw's mother used to have dreams all the time, but she knew what they were. You 'member that story, Em, about the doctor? Out in the field?

EMILY. The one about the accident?

LIZ. Grandmomma woke Grandpoppa up in the dead of night. Said, "Get up, Jasper, and hitch up the mules. Dr. Payne needs me."

EMILY. [explaining to HALLIE] Dr. Payne was a country doctor that she helped out sometimes, kind of like a nurse.

HALLIE. He was a *doctor* and his name was *PAIN*?

EMILY. P-A-Y-N-E. But I know. Funny, idn't it?

27

LIZ. I once knew a dentist named Chip. [*then returning to the story at hand*] 'Course, Mamaw's mother wasn't really his nurse, either; just a good midwife and helper who knew folk remedies and things.

EMILY. Anyway, she'd had this dream about a wagon accident somewhere out in a pasture over by where they lived.

LIZ. No, now, I thought it happened in one of their own fields.

EMILY. Nuh-uh. It was on up the road. Over toward Yellow Dog, I b'lieve. She woke up in the dark, already knowing just which farm to go to and pretty much what had happened out there.

HALLIE. Are you telling me she was psychic?

LIZ. You could call it that. She didn't know to.

HALLIE. But she could really know the future?

LIZ. Sometimes the future. Sometimes the present, happening someplace else. It's hard to say how the gift of the Sight works. Usually with her, she'd have a dream and when she woke up she'd know just what to do.

EMILY. She said she could see it so plain in her dream ... the wagon turned over, a boy hurt on the ground, people standing around holding lanterns, and the doctor's instruments all laid out, unrolled in this canvas pouch he carried them in. In the dream, she could see every single one of those tools – individually. Said when she got out there, it all looked <u>exactly</u> the way she had dreamed it.

LIZ. Just exactly.

HALLIE. Huh.

LIZ. Yep.

HALLIE. How often did this sort of thing happen?

LIZ. Wagon accidents? Oh, not all that often.

HALLIE. No, no – this vision thing, or this dreaming, or whatever it was.

LIZ. Oh, all the time, I s'pose. Pretty regular. There's lots of stories.

HALLIE. How come I never heard 'em?

EMILY. Running wild outside chasin' lightnin' bugs with your cousins all your life, probably—instead of sittin' around the kitchen table listenin' to the tales old folks tell.

HALLIE. What else did she see?

LIZ. Well, there's one time she woke up early one Saturday morning and told Grandpoppa to get the wagon hitched, that they had to go 'cross the river to Cairo [pronounced KAY-ro] to meet the twins at the train depot. 'Course, there hadn't been any mention of this event until that very moment — no news that these twins were coming for a visit.

HALLIE. What twins were these?

LIZ. I don't remember ever knowing. Some of her nieces who lived off up north — Illinois or Wisconsin, I b'lieve. Maybe children of one of her cousins? Can't say for sure.

EMILY. But Grandmomma said she had dreamed they were coming that very day on the noon train. And Grandpoppa Jasper, having gone through this kind of thing time and again with her, neither argued nor batted an eye. When she said to hitch up the team, well, he just headed to the barn and he hitched.

LIZ. Wasn't any _need_ to argue with her. He knew by then that when she'd had a vision, she was always right.

EMILY. So they left for Cairo real early that morning. Went across the bridge — or it might have been a ferry back in those days. Anyway, they got to the depot ...

LIZ. ... and when that noon train pulled in ...

EMILY. ... by golly, off stepped those twins!

HALLIE. But that's just ....

EMILY. Didn't come as a surprise to Grandmomma, nor to Grandpoppa Jasper either, for that matter.

HALLIE. Lord, what if they hadn't gone to meet the train that morning?

EMILY. Well, think about it — this was long ago and those two little girls were from far enough off that they'd have been in a terrible predicament if they had traveled hundreds of miles just to be left stranded, not knowing a soul, at this strange depot. No telephones ...

HALLIE. But _how_ did she know? And how did she know it would be the _noon_ train?

LIZ. It's the Sight, I'm telling you. She had these dreams, and she learned to trust them.

EMILY. Funny thing is ... about a week later a letter arrived. It was from the twins' mother up north. Postmark was a month old, but somehow the letter hadn't made it

29

to Grandmomma on time.

LIZ. The letter said to please meet the noon train in Cairo on such-and-such-a-date ... that the twins would be coming for a visit.

HALLIE. You have _got_ to be kidding me.

[_rapid fire delivery:_] LIZ. No, ma'am.

                HALLIE. No way!

                EMILY. Yes way.

                LIZ. Yes, ma'am.

HALLIE. This is incredible. It's like something you read in a book or see in a movie. Like ... like one of those stories in Ripley's, or whatever.

EMILY. Well, it wasn't. It was real. And from Grandmomma, our Mamaw inherited the same gift. She had the Sight too.

HALLIE. Mamaw had these kinds of visions?

EMILY. She sure did.

LIZ. Oh, Emmers, tell about that time with the hobo.

EMILY. [_to HALLIE_] You even know what a hobo is?

HALLIE. Nuh-uh.

EMILY. Well, it's what people used to call wanderers – men during the Great Depression who stole rides all around the country on freight trains looking for work.

LIZ. They would hop into these train boxcars and go from town to town hunting jobs, because work was so scarce. Sometimes whole groups of them would camp out in the train yards waiting for rides. Called their camps "hobo jungles." People wrote songs about 'em and everything. [_an anticipatory beat_] The Great Depression? Ring a bell?

HALLIE. This was when? 1930s?

LIZ. That's right. [_to EMILY_] Looks like they _are_ teaching her something in that new schoolhouse up there in town after all.

EMILY. Our tax nickels at work.

HALLIE. I watched it on the History Channel, that's all. [_prompting them to continue_] Anyway ...

EMILY. Anyway, these hobos would sometimes wander up to people's doors asking to do odd jobs in exchange for food.

HALLIE. Eww.

LIZ. No, they did this all the time. People were used to it. It was hard times for the whole country. A lot of folks were troubled, and people like Mamaw were always willing to help somebody out with a meal.

EMILY. The hobos were mostly just regular people that had hit a patch of rough luck.

LIZ. Real rough luck. Down and out, as they say. If one of 'em found a house that was hobo-friendly, he would put a certain mark on the gatepost so others would know.

EMILY. They put certain other marks on unfriendly places.

HALLIE. You mean sort of a hobo code system?

LIZ. Something like that.

EMILY. Mamaw and Grandpaw were a young couple then. They had a friendly mark on their gatepost because she was known to feed hungry folks that stopped by.

LIZ. Well, one day ...

EMILY. [with a tone of 'I'm-telling-this-story!'] ... One day, this man came around to the back here, knocked, and she went over from whatever she was doing to speak to him through the screen door. Said he hadn't eaten that day and offered to chop up her kindling if she'd feed him a meal. Well she said, 'Sure." So he went about chopping up what little stove wood there was out there while she fixed him a ham biscuit. He didn't work long, she said, because she'd n'more than got that ham biscuit together but he was back at the screen door. So, she picked up the food, stepped over to the door, and said she was just reaching out to push it open when she got the worst feeling of her life ... and a dream she'd had the week before flashed in front of her.

LIZ. [Acting out the action] Instead of pushing the screen door open, she — quick! — hooked the latch and reached back for the big wooden door, standing open beside her.

EMILY. And just as she was slamming it, she saw [acting out the action] that man's knife slash down through the screen wire.

HALLIE. What the...?!

LIZ. That had been her dream! Said she'd seen it before ... that very picture. Had dreamed a man tried to stab her with a big knife through a screen door.

EMILY. And she remembered the dream just in time!

LIZ. Well, it scared her half to death ...

EMILY. ... naturally! So she ran around in the house fast as she could, bolted the front door and closed all the windows. Then she watched him from behind the front room curtain. Said he went on down the road in kind of a hurry.

HALLIE. Lord, if she hadn't had that dream ... !

EMILY. If she hadn't remembered having it! Just in the nick!

LIZ. I guess he didn't get whatever it was that he really came for, so he decided to beat it out of there.

HALLIE. But what if he had?! What if he'd killed her?!

LIZ. Then, my dear, we wouldn't be here today, would we?

HALLIE. [with a tone of wonder] Well, I'll be.

EMILY. But look here, Hallie — Mamaw didn't let that one incident stop her from feeding people. She never did see that man again, but she still fed every hobo that came to her door from that day until the Depression finally let up.

LIZ. I think she kept the door latched all the time for a while there, though.

HALLIE. Do you blame her? I would too.

EMILY. It only stands to reason.

HALLIE. So, you're saying you think she got these ... these powers from her mother? Inherited them, so to speak?

LIZ. Well, why not? I mean, if you can look at a child and say he has his mother's green eyes, or she has her Aunt Minnie's earlobes, or great-granddaddy's curly black hair, then why not something that's not physical? Why couldn't you be given snatches of their thoughts and memories too?

HALLIE. You're saying you think people can get personality traits and skills and things by ... by heredity?

LIZ. Look — haven't you ever heard somebody say, "That boy has his Uncle Fred's sense of humor"? Well, that's not physical, is it? And yet, you know exactly what that means. You've seen that in our own family. Or how about somebody who is a natural at something ... like woodworking, or making up songs and stories? It's like they don't even have to learn how to do it — they're just born good at it from the start.

EMILY. [pondering a new possibility] And what about déjà vu?

HALLIE. Huh?

EMILY. Think about it.

LIZ. [catching on and considering this new idea] Hmmm. Now that's an interesting twist, cousin.

EMILY. It seems like a pretty complicated area, is all I'm saying.

HALLIE. What does déjà vu have to do with any of this?

EMILY. What do you think?

HALLIE. Inheriting traits ... [thinking hard, counting off clues

32

on her fingers, trying to put it all together] ... curly hair, gift of the sight, sense of humor. *[confused]* And déjà vu? *[an epiphany]* Déjà vu! When you feel like you've seen something before! But ... but it might actually be a piece of someone else's memory that you, maybe, <u>inherited</u> — is that it?

EMILY. That's what I'm wondering, is all.

HALLIE. Spooky.

EMILY. You think so?

HALLIE. Of course! *[with a dismissive gesture]* You guys are bordering on scary. This is weird stuff.

EMILY. Well, it doesn't scare me. Could be the reason we see the world or life in certain ways ... and don't know why.

LIZ. Yeah. Say you are attracted to certain 'foreign' foods or have a nagging need to travel to a particular place ...

HALLIE. Or if you think you ... *[she stops abruptly]*

EMILY. What, honey?

HALLIE. *[hesitantly]* If you think maybe you hear a voice that you <u>know</u> you somehow know, even though there's no one there.

LIZ. Are you saying ...?

HALLIE. I'm not saying anything. I'm just asking.

EMILY. What does the voice say to you, Hallie?

HALLIE. It says, "Hallie Linn." Nobody ever calls me by my whole name. I hear the voice, though, just as if it were right beside me. It's not my imagination, either. I know what that sounds like inside my head. I know the difference. And I'm NOT crazy.

EMILY. Of course you're not. Is it a man's voice or a woman's?

HALLIE. A woman. An older woman.

LIZ. When do you hear this voice?

HALLIE. Important times. Like the time I fell out of the barn loft and broke my leg in two places. I lay there and cried. I was so scared, and it hurt so bad. I didn't know if anyone would ever find me, and I couldn't walk to get help. I heard it then: "Hallie Linn, be still. They'll be here in a little while. Wait, honey." And this perfect calm came over me. I quit worrying all at once, and my leg didn't even hurt until they picked me up later on. I just lay there and waited and felt

33

safe.

EMILY. Is it always the same voice?

HALLIE. When I hear it, it's always the same. But sometimes I don't hear the voice; I just feel something ... a kind of a ... presence, I guess you'd call it. Usually when something bad has happened but we don't know it yet.

LIZ. Like a prediction?

HALLIE. Kind of, I s'pose. Only I don't usually know specifically what it's about. I have this peculiar feeling and then a _knowing_ comes over me. I just _know_. Someone close to me has troubles. Big troubles. I feel real sad ... and also jittery, like I want to do something but I don't know who to go to. I get it in my stomach. I had that feeling the night my dad's truck ran off the bridge into the creek, before we found out about the wreck.

[_LIZ looks at EMILY._]

HALLIE. And I had it today. Which is why I came over here.

[_EMILY looks at LIZ._]

LIZ. [_after a beat or two_] Well, here we all are, and everybody's fine.

EMILY. Could be you've got it, Hal.

HALLIE. Got what?

EMILY. The gift.

LIZ. Maybe it was in your stars. Could be you got it from Mamaw and from her mother — stamped right on your genes, girl.

HALLIE. Holy moly.

EMILY. [_Looks at LIZ, considers HALLIE for a beat or two_] You weren't but about 5 years old.

HALLIE. Huh?

EMILY. When she died.

HALLIE. S'cuse me?

EMILY. But you were the one who knew.

HALLIE. What're we talking about now? Some more of your old ghost stuff?

LIZ. "And a little child will lead them."

EMILY. That very morning you told your momma not to worry ... that the angels were coming to get Mamaw. You said, "They'll come by and get her tonight, and then she won't feel bad anymore."

HALLIE. _I_ said that? You know, I barely remember Mamaw.

34

But I do a little. Remember her.

LIZ. You were the sweetest little thing that ever was in this world.

EMILY. Your momma came over here to Mamaw's house around noon that day. This was after the stroke. She and Pearl were here in the kitchen. Pearl was peeling potatoes for supper, I b'lieve your momma said, and Mamaw was sitting there keeping her company. Your momma said she went to the little store that used to be up the road, to pick up three pork chops, and before she could get from the meat counter to the checkout, they told her Pearl was on the phone asking for her. And Pearl said to her, said, "Honey, come home." That's all she said, and hung up, and your momma knew it was bad.

LIZ. By the time she got back here, Doc Bracken was already in the back bedroom there, trying ever'thing he could think of to save Mamaw.

EMILY. Said she and Pearl could see him through the doorway, working over her. Said she'd never seen anybody work so hard. He tried and he tried, she said...

LIZ. But, of course, there wasn't anything ....

EMILY. ... wasn't anything he could do.

LIZ. She was gone. Her heart.

EMILY. Her great old big, tender heart. It finally just gave out.

HALLIE. [voicing wonder] The angels came.

EMILY. Well, Pearl had a temporary come-apart, Mamaw being her last living sibling, and all. But later on that evening when everything was calmer, your momma drove home. And she said you walked off of your all's porch and across the yard, right up to her car door. Said you took her by the hand as she climbed out, and you looked up at her face and smiled and said, "The angels came by, didn't they, Mommy? See, I told you they would."

HALLIE. I ... I don't ...

EMILY. You weren't but a little bitty thing.

HALLIE. But how could ... how did ...?

LIZ. Maybe you've got the gift of the Sight. Maybe you've just not known how to use it.

HALLIE. The gift of ...?

LIZ. That's something, isn't it?

EMILY. Hallie, honey, you all right?
HALLIE. [*trying to take it all in; a bit confused.*] Fine. Fine.
I just came by to see about y'all. [*Pulls out her cell phone.*]
Let me check in with Daddy. I'll be back out in a minute.

[*Lights fade slowly as HALLIE absorbs what she's just
learned. After a beat, she dials her dad and enters the
house.*]
[*Lights down.*]

SCENE 5

[*Lights come up slowly. Scene is <u>outside</u> same farmhouse at
<u>night</u>, <u>circa 1900</u>. Light bulb is no longer hanging in the
window. There is a dim glow from a lantern inside. Because
the house is newer, the porch is in considerably better condition; flowers, rather than weeds, grow near the steps. The
porch holds functional objects indicating everyday life of
the period. Characters are dressed in period clothing.*]

[*The small body, lying on the kitchen table and covered by
a sheet, is visible through the window.*]

[*ANNIE sits in moonlight on the two low steps. Without
much enthusiasm, she begins breaking beans into a bowl
and sadly <u>humming</u> the traditional country hymn "Farther
Along." She begins to <u>sing</u> the chorus.*]

ANNIE. [*<u>sings</u>*] "Farther along we'll / know all about it /
farther along we'll / understand why .... Cheer up my
sister / live in the sunshine / we'll understand it / all by
and by ...."

[*TESS moves to the open window inside the kitchen and
listens through the screen. As the song progresses, TESS
moves to the unopened screen door and softly hums the
harmony part. ANNIE notices her, nods and offers a small
smile. TESS does not respond.*]
[*After another chorus, this time with ANNIE <u>singing</u> lyrics
and TESS quietly and tentatively <u>singing</u> the harmony and
wiping her eyes occasionally, ANNIE pauses.*]
ANNIE. Come on out here and sing it with me, honey.
[*TESS shakes her head, moves away from the door back*

36

through the kitchen to window.]

ANNIE. Oh, come on, Tess. Let's try it together. We need to.

TESS. *[speaks quietly through the open window]* Not now, Annie.

ANNIE. Well, when, Tess? We should practice it. Tomorrow we won't have a chance. They'll all be getting here.

[TESS reaches for the thin window curtains and pulls them together slowly, then exits to one side toward the house's implied "front rooms" offstage.]

[ANNIE sighs, sits gazing at the stars, hands idle in the bean bowl. Begins to hum "Farther Along" again, solo. Wipes her eyes; goes back to breaking beans.]
[Lights fade.]

SCENE 6

[Scene is <u>inside</u> kitchen of the farmhouse, <u>morning</u>. <u>The present</u>. Window curtains are parted. Unlit light bulb hangs in window. LIZ is seated at the table with her head in her hands.]

EMILY enters from the implied "front rooms" of the house. She crosses to LIZ, leans down from behind her, and wraps her in a hug.]

EMILY. You gonna be okay?

LIZ. To be honest? I just do not know.

EMILY. Talk to me, cousin.

LIZ. It's Dad. I guess I just don't know where I went wrong.

EMILY. Where *you* went wrong??

LIZ. Here we are, doing this thing — and I understand that it has to be done — but it just makes me feel like ... I don't know ... like a traitor, I guess.

EMILY. Traitor? You? Liz, it's not you that's been the traitor of this family. Surely you know that.

LIZ. He's such a mess, and I know it. He's done some horrible things ... to all of us. He drinks; he .... But he's still...

EMILY. ... your daddy.

LIZ. He is. And all my life — what little of it he was around — I remember him always talking about how if he only had

37

a place like this of his own, he could ... I think he thought
he could change his life. Fix it all somehow.

EMILY. And what's that got to do with now?

LIZ. Here I've been in a position to help him have his
dream ... his shot at making a better life ... or at least
at finding some peace. And I just couldn't bring him in.
Or maybe I could've and I just didn't.

EMILY. Or maybe it turned out this way because he
wasn't ever around, wasn't ever here for you. That was _his_
choice.

LIZ. He's still my daddy.

EMILY. Liz, now listen to me. You had no say in this. I
mean, I know he's your daddy and all, but there's not a
soul in this family – not _one_ – who would agree to be in-
volved in any kind of business deal with Gary. Not property, not money, nothing. To a person, there's not a single
one of us in this family who would predict anything but
failure and ruin in such an arrangement. He's, as you say,
done too much damage. It'd be hard – and stupid – to
trust him. And I know you're not stupid. I've got to tell you
that _I_ would _never_ agree to trusting him. Not after all the
water that's flowed under the bridge these many years.

LIZ. But, Emily, he's my dad! All I ever wanted was ...

EMILY. Yes.

LIZ. Maybe he broke people's hearts because his was
broken somehow a long time ago. If I could just figure
out what it was, how to get through to him .... I mean, I
wanted to. I tried.

EMILY. You did.

LIZ. But maybe I didn't try enough. Or hard enough.

EMILY. You did, Liz.

LIZ. Some people say it's an illness. A kind of disease.

EMILY. And some people who are sick work real hard to
get themselves treated. Uncle Gary never has. In fact, as
far as I know, he's spent most of his life cussing anybody
that even suggested he might have a problem.

LIZ. Dammit. Dammit! All to _hell_! I HATE this. It makes me
sick right in my stomach. Yet life, somehow, always goes
right along ... in spite of every damned thing.

EMILY. I know, honey. But you know: "never the same river
twice." Still it's almost too much to know and still hold up

under.

[*A beat as they ponder.*]

LIZ. Did my daddy ever love me, Em? Do you think? 'Cause I really don't know.

EMILY. Sure he did. How could he not love lovable you? Sweet girl. But Gary's problem always was that he loved that damned bottle, too. And he let it get in between him and love. In between him and reason, him and family. It definitely got in between him and the law. And I'll tell you what I think ... I think he let it get in between him and himself. And that, combined with his unchecked ego, <u>turned</u> him ... a long time ago. There wasn't anything you could do about that. Not a living thing.

LIZ. I gotta go wash my face.

[*LIZ exits.*]

EMILY. [*calling after LIZ*] You were only a kid, Lizzy.

[*HALLIE nears the porch, apparently having been out for a run.*]

HALLIE. Anybody home?

[*HALLIE enters through the screen door.*]

EMILY. Morning, Hal.

HALLIE. Where's Liz?

EMILY. She'll be down in a few minutes.

[*HALLIE opens the cooler, gets out a bottle of orange juice, uncaps it and takes a swig.*]

HALLIE. Anything wrong?

EMILY. Hallie, do you actually remember Uncle Gary?

HALLIE. [*thinks hard*] You mean Liz's dad?

EMILY. That's him. Do you?

HALLIE. Not really. I know him mostly from photos. But from what I've heard, I haven't missed much.

EMILY. He's been gone from here a long time. Prob'ly since you were pretty small.

HALLIE. I heard he was in prison.

EMILY. It's not the first time. He's stayed in trouble all his life, just about. He drinks. Picks fights. It's kept Liz torn up for years.

HALLIE. Is he out?

EMILY. He's out.

HALLIE. Does she see him?

EMILY. She's not heard from him yet.

39

HALLIE. That must be tough. Not knowing where he is.

EMILY. Yeah, it is. She feels like he's at loose ends and it's her fault.

HALLIE. How's she figure that?

EMILY. I think she believes that if she could just get him close enough, she could make him stop drinking and acting a fool. Breaking the law. Pissing everybody off.

HALLIE. You mean she wants him to move in with her?

EMILY. Not necessarily. She hasn't ever felt close to him. She knows he's disconnected with everybody, but she can't understand why he wouldn't want to at least <u>try</u> to connect with his own daughter.

HALLIE. Why's he such a loner anyway?

EMILY. I've never known. But I do know that he somehow got stuck ... never really grew up, if you know what I mean. They say drinking will do that to a person. Or may- be drinking is the symptom. Either way, he's been at it most of his life. Liz doesn't know this, but some of us think it's what drove her mom to an early grave.

[LIZ enters.]

LIZ. *[to HALLIE]* You're up early, kiddo.

HALLIE. In my limited experience, I have found that it's better to run before the heat of the day.

LIZ. *[sarcastically]* Even better not to run at all.

HALLIE. Such an optimist. One more reason to adore you, old auntie.

LIZ. Who're you calling old?!

HALLIE. Speaking of which ... what's with the funeral flowers out there on the front porch?

EMILY. *[looking at LIZ]* Is it today already?

LIZ. Oh! I can't believe I'd forgotten.

EMILY. Did you hear him this morning?

LIZ. Never did. I guess he must have stopped by b'fore we woke up. And I haven't been out front yet.

HALLIE. Who? What's up?

LIZ. Your Great-uncle Furman. He does this every year at this time. Leaves flowers on Mamaw's front steps. Says it's the best way to remember.

HALLIE. What's he remembering, then?

LIZ. Why, the day his mother died.

EMILY. They were so close. It's so sad.

40

LIZ. He never could bear the thought of visiting her grave at the cemetery. Said that's not where she is nor ever was. Said if she's anywhere, she's right here where she belongs. At home.

HALLIE. But nobody lives here.

LIZ. That's not what he maintains.

HALLIE. Are you telling me ....?

EMILY. He leaves flowers here at the house the way some people leave them at the cemetery on Decoration Day. Isn't that sweet? And sad.

HALLIE. Sounds a little bit strange to me.

LIZ. Now, baby, don't you ever judge another person's heart. Furman's is good. He cain't hardly stand it that she's gone — our Mamaw, his own sweet mother — so he deals with it in his own way. And if leaving her a bouquet of flowers on her front steps every April 22 for the past 15 years makes him feel better, who are we to say otherwise?

EMILY. He's never set one single foot in that graveyard since the day we took her there. Says he never will.

HALLIE. Whatever.

EMILY. Don't be mean-spirited, Hallie. It's just not like you.

LIZ. Furman is good, and he loves _you_ and _us_ and ever'body in this family, and you'd do well not to ever forget that, little missy. He's been good to you.

HALLIE. Well, what do you want me to say?

EMILY. If you cain't say something nice, then I'd suggest...

EMILY & LIZ. ...don't say anything at all!

HALLIE. [rolling her eyes] You're killing me dead. You really and truly are.

[Lights fade.]

SCENE 7

[Lights up. Scene is _outside_ same farmhouse, _early evening_. _The present_. The kitchen window is open, as usual. The unlit bulb hangs in the window.]

[HALLIE is sitting on the porch, hyper-focused on rummaging through a box of photographs and objects, some of which lie around the box. She finds a yellowed news clipping and begins to read it silently.]

41

[EMILY enters and lays her hand gently on HALLIE's shoulder as she passes her.]

EMILY. I'm sure glad you decided to stay out here with us, Hallie. We'll pop us some popcorn after supper, just like Mamaw used to do for Liz and me in the old days. That sound good to you?

HALLIE. *[not looking up]* Uh-huh. Fine.

EMILY. Well, don't get all excited.

HALLIE. Oh, I'm sorry, Aunt Emmers. I'm just preoccupied. This stuff is incredible.

EMILY. I have often said that we are most likely to find our history ... and therefore ourselves ... while digging in a soft pasteboard box. It's modern archeology. You "dig"?

HALLIE. *[sarcastically]* Ha. You ever think about writing a book?

EMILY. Not I, my dear. Were I ever to let our skeletons hear me creeping about the closet door, they'd break it down and trample me to pieces. Nope, I think I'll leave that little joy for you someday.

HALLIE. Scaredy cat. *[holds out two silver coins]* Hey, have you ever seen these? They're really old.

EMILY. *[taking the coins and reaching for her glasses hanging from a cord around her neck]* Yes, I have. Is the note still in there?

HALLIE. Note?

EMILY. *[pointing to the box]* There used to be a letter some-where in there that stayed with these coins. Written on pale blue paper edged in black?

HALLIE. *[digging, locating something]* Is this it?

EMILY. Could be. What does it say?

HALLIE. *[reading]* 'Monday Morning. Dearest Tess. We just received the sad news. Place these coins on Auntie when you prepare her for her reward. I have been saving them these past few years — they are the same used on little William Edward. I hope you have not already used copper coins, for they will cause the skin to turn green. I am sending these across the way by Lily, as you can see, and the rest of us will be along early this afternoon, after tolling the church bell. We think it is 89 times, and I hope to the Lord that that is the right number of her years. Don't forget to lay a rag soaked

in soda water over the face to keep its color from turn-
ing. Drop aspirin on it every once in a while, for that will
help too. Was she able to finish sewing her burial gown?
You did right to keep the hatchet under her bed to cut her
pain. Well, God bless us every one. What will we ever do
without her? You have been a saint to keep her so well for
so long. When you get to heaven, there will be stars in your
crown. Affectionately, Annie.'

EMILY. That's the one.

HALLIE. But what were the coins for? Who are these people?

EMILY. Long time ago when someone died, it was up to the
family to get the deceased ready for burial. There weren't
any funeral parlors or undertakers, except in town. Around
here, we took care of our own. I was born too late to
remember this, of course, but I remember hearing Mamaw
talking about it.

HALLIE. And the coins?

EMILY. They were for the eyelids – to keep them shut.

HALLIE. Oh, my god. And the hatchet?

EMILY. Oh, that was just superstition. They believed that
since a hatchet could cut things, maybe it could somehow
"cut" the pain.

HALLIE. What??

EMILY. [dismissively] Yeah. Anyway. The women would
prepare the corpse … they called it 'washing the body.'
They had to do this quickly, before rigor mortis set in.
Otherwise, they'd have to break limb bones to position
them and to get the burial clothes on.

HALLIE. Good lord.

[LIZ enters]

EMILY. They said after a person died, it was hard to do
anything with the corpse once it got stiff and swollen. They
had to work fast. I think they used to take the dresses or
pants or whatever and split them up the back sometimes, to
get them on the body. Maybe they still do, for all I know.

HALLIE. That's awful. [to LIZ] Don't you think that's awful?

LIZ. Not so awful.

EMILY. Naw, not really. Ooh, I've even heard them tell
about massaging the cheeks to get the eyes to close! One
time I heard them say a woman who was washing her

43

husband's body found a great long scar across his back that she had never known was there.

HALLIE. No way.

EMILY. It was different times, Hal. Just think about having to wash the body of your own parent, sibling, spouse ... anyone you loved so dear.

HALLIE. I couldn't do it.

EMILY. Oh, you _would_. You'd have to. Who else would there be to do it? And, too, they wanted to make everything nice for the sitting up. Wanted to make the corpse look presentable.

HALLIE. [_makes a face_] Ooo.

EMILY. I know. I used to cringe when they'd tell it.

LIZ. But, being a child with a morbid curiosity, you'd beg to hear it anyway.

EMILY. Hush, you.

LIZ. It's true.

HALLIE. And the 'sitting up'?

EMILY. That's what they called it. Like a wake or a visitation. People would sit up with the body all through the night, every night until the burial.

HALLIE. To keep away the ghost, or what?

EMILY. No, honey. Just out of respect. Nothing spooky about it. Except one time I heard about a corpse that sat straight up in its coffin. It was the wee hours. Like to have scared the people sitting up half to death!

HALLIE. I guess so!

LIZ. Cleared the room, they said!

HALLIE. [_overlapping LIZ_] I'd have torn right through the screen door!

EMILY. [_laughing at HALLIE's reaction_] It was just a rigor mortis reaction, though. 'Course, they _thought_ he had come back to life on them! One of them ran out into the yard hollering for whiskey. Another one dropped to his knees on the front porch and got saved on the spot! That's how they tell it.

HALLIE. Ha!

EMILY. My mother used to say that, most likely, when the end of the world is nigh, the sinners will be the ones praying and saints will be the ones sinning ... before it's too late!

HALLIE. Barbaric!

44

EMILY. Big word! No, this is just the way people lived around here back then, Hallie. It wasn't unusual or frightening to them. They did what they had to do. They washed the body — they were careful; they were reverent. Kind of like Jesus washing his disciples' feet in the book of John. It was terribly sad for the family, of course. But to let their loved ones go unwashed would have been unthinkable. To have ignored their last wishes or to have buried them soiled or in everyday clothes would have been blasphemous. They went into the ground in the very best that they had, all cleaned up and prepared to enter heaven, I reckon. Had to get 'em ready for going up 'home.'

HALLIE. [pulling her feet up into the chair she sitting in] Sooooo ... where are they buried?

EMILY. [laughing] Don't worry, honey. They're not underneath your feet! Most of 'em ... [laughs at HALLIE's horrified expression] Most of 'em are restin' peaceful in the churchyard.

HALLIE. [looking over the letter] And who was "little William Edward"?

EMILY. [taking the letter and looking at it] Don't recall ever knowing. Must've been a young cousin or uncle of ours 'way back. Hmmm. Guess he must have died young.

HALLIE. You mean it's some dead person that was kin to us?

EMILY. [chuckles] Well, there's a lot more of our kin that are dead than alive.

HALLIE. But still ...

EMILY. Seems like I vaguely remember hearing Mamaw talk about one of her great-aunts having a baby or a toddler or something that died under curious circumstances. [struggling to recall] What was that? I can't get it to come back to me. Something about a sudden death. Accident, not illness. This was so long ago, even *I* can't remember — so, honey, you know that's an old, old story! Still, I wish I could call it to mind ...

HALLIE. All this death stuff is too much ... something. Creepy, I guess.

EMILY. Well, why don't we give it a rest, then? That hall closet at the head of the stairs needs emptying. Not much in there, but you could finish it off, and that would be the last thing up there to do.

HALLIE. Okay, but don't get rid of this box. I want to look at the rest of these letters and things later on.

EMILY. Mamaw would be proud to know that somebody cares about these old things she held onto over the years. Meanwhile, young lady, we're runnin' out of time around here. We've got to get the rest of this old castle polished and shined before they all get here tomorrow. Now, can we get back to it, please?

HALLIE. [teasing] Slave driver.

EMILY. Slug.

HALLIE. You're only a big fish in this little pond — you know that, don't you?

EMILY. Why, thanks for pointing that out to me, Bait.

HALLIE. [grinning] My pleasure. [HALLIE turns to go.]

EMILY. Hey?

HALLIE. Huh?

EMILY. I'm awfully glad you're here for this, Hallie-M'lallie. Makes it go down a little easier.

[EMILY blows a kiss; HALLIE pretends to catch it, then exits.]
[Lights fade.]

SCENE 8

[Lights up. Scene is inside and outside same farmhouse kitchen. Night. Characters wear period clothing, except HALLIE. There is a dim light from a lantern hanging in the open kitchen window. The house is quiet. HALLIE is alone at the picnic table in the yard, slumped in profile, asleep on her folded arms. The pasteboard box and its contents are spread around her. Her cellphone lies nearby. A clock ticks.]

[As if from a great distance, TESS's and ANNIE's voices are heard. ANNIE is singing low (a hymn); TESS is crying.]

[HALLIE rustles in her sleep, turns her head so she now faces downstage (away from the upcoming TESS and ANNIE scene, which crosses time), but HALLIE does not wake from this dream.]

[Light rises in the kitchen. ANNIE sits in the kitchen, quilting. Peaceful but sorrowful, she hums/sings to herself. Occasionally, she wipes her eyes. Occasionally, she speaks to the corpse.]

ANNIE. Don't worry, baby boy. Don't you worry, little Will.
Mama's here with you. Mama's here. [She resumes *humming.*]
[*TESS enters, jolted to find Annie there, alone with the corpse.*]
TESS. I ... I'm sorry. [*She turns to exit.*]
ANNIE. No, Tess. Please. Stay.
TESS. I ... I just can't, Annie. And don't be sweet to me.
I don't deserve it.
ANNIE. Tessie, you are my own and only sister. You are my
heart. Please — don't torture yourself.
TESS. But it's my fault. I'm the one to blame, and I *can* not
bear it.
ANNIE. Dear Tess ....
TESS. How can you even look at me?! Why insist on forgiving
me when *I* can't? *God* shouldn't even forgive me, Annie. I'm the
worst person on the face of the earth, and if I could die in this
child's place, I *would*!
ANNIE. I know, darling Tess. As would I. But dearest, we can't.
Our lot is to carry this burden.
TESS. Annie, you would have this precious child playing in your
lap instead of lying here like this, if not for me.
ANNIE. Tess. Do you hear me? You did *not* do this.
TESS. Oh, but I did. Yet ... where is my punishment?
ANNIE. Love, it is right there in your heart. You have created
your own punishment. God already forgives you. Now, you
must forgive yourself.
TESS. But do *you* forgive me, Annie? *How* can you?
ANNIE. Forgive you? For what, Tess? For being a loving
sister to me? For loving my child since the day he was born?
For caring for him as if he were your own? What is it that I
should forgive, Tessie my love? Your pure heart? You have not
wronged me.
TESS. You know what for, Annie! I *killed* your *child*. My own
sister's sweet boy. He lies there because of me.
ANNIE. He lies there because Nature is cruel. But there is no
cruelty in *you*, Sister.
TESS. Please, God, let me die in his place! Let me go for him!
[*dissolves into anguish, kneeling next to Annie's chair, head in
Annie's lap*]
ANNIE. [*strokes TESS's hair, comforting her*] Oh, Tessie, it could
as easily have been me. Don't blame yourself, baby sister.
Annie's here with you. It will all be made right.

[ANNIE resumes singing/humming; looks sadly past the top of TESS's head toward the corpse.]

ANNIE. This was my child who loved me. He depended on me. And I will not let him go to his reward with any trouble in his soul. I won't have him worry throughout eternity that you are burdened because of him. Tessie, listen to me. He loved you, and he adored you. And because you loved him too, you must help him to move on without this tribulation. _Tell him_, Tess.

TESS. [between sobs] Little Will, I'm so very sorry and ashamed. I will gladly go instead, if you'll make it so. This is my own horrible fault. Oh, Willie, I should have been more careful. I should never have let my eyes stray from you. Not for one second.

ANNIE. That's the way. Just speak what's on your heart. He hears you.

[ANNIE now begins to cry silently.]

TESS. I loved you from the first minute I laid eyes on you, so tiny and soft. So sweet smelling. And so _loud_! [TESS and ANNIE share a smile through tears] I have loved you almost as much as your own dear mother has loved you. And, child, I love you still.

[TESS becomes calmer as she talks. Eventually, her grief releases her, and she is able to become the comforter to ANNIE, who, in turn, is finally able to let go and grieve.]

TESS. Forgive me my terrible deed, my sweet Sweet-William. I let that News Bee distract me from you, and in a blink ... in a blink ... you are gone. I was your keeper, and I failed you. Such a blessing, our dear boy. A joy to your mother. It's because of the goodness in you that you've been chosen an angel.

[ANNIE sobs over the corpse in utter anguish]

TESS. We will carry him in our hearts, Annie. He'll watch over us. And some day, Sister, if time is good to us, we will again learn to rest. There now. You cry. I'm here.

[ANNIE sobs. TESS comforts her.]

TESS: Annie, they'll all be coming tomorrow. We'll need to be ready.

[TESS begins to hum and then sing "Farther Along" as _kitchen light_ fades to black and singing fades away.]

HALLIE. [Awakens into silence with a start.] Tess?

[*then, more quietly*] Tess.
[*HALLIE looks up at the house, searching the darkness. She runs to exit into the house.*]
[*Lights fade.*]

SCENE 9

[*Scene is* <u>outside</u> *kitchen of same farmhouse,* <u>night</u>. <u>The present</u>. *The stage is empty. Windows and curtains are open; light bulb unlit. The figure of a disheveled man about 70 (GARY) crosses the porch, peers in through the windows, crosses to door and reaches above the exterior doorframe, feeling for something. He finds the* <u>skeleton</u> <u>key</u>, *then exits through the yard, taking the key with him.*]
[*Blackout.*]

~ END OF ACT I ~

ACT II

SCENE 1

*[Scene is _inside_ same farmhouse kitchen, _late morning_. The
present. Light bulb, unlit, hangs in the window. Lively "hoe-
down" music plays on a radio, as the cousins get things ready
for the family gathering.]*

*[EMILY and LIZ are stirring about hastily, wringing out
cleaning rags, placing the last of the bottles and cans of
various cleaning solutions into a bucket, tying up a trash bag.
The cousins begin taking food and utensils out of a cooler,
boxes and sacks. They move back and forth quickly between
the kitchen, the picnic table, and the porch table during the
dialogue.]*

*[HALLIE, sleepy-eyed, enters and is given a job to do in
preparation for the day's coming events.]*

LIZ. *[to HALLIE]* Well, would you look at what the cat
dragged in! *[hands something to HALLIE to get her involved]*
Here you go, missy!
*[HALLIE begins helping. She hum or sings a couple lines of
the hymn "Farther Along" as she works.]*
EMILY. *[to LIZ]* Lord have mercy, here we are at D-Day.
Reckon we're ready?
LIZ. I'll never be ready. Never.
EMILY. We're ready. Have to be. They'll all be gettin' here
soon. Best lay out the food.
LIZ. Cold fried chicken — you know that's one of _my_
favorites. Makes a good picnic. Did you sweep the dog-
wood blossoms off the old table out in the side yard?
EMILY. Yes'm, Miss Bossy-Behind. _And_ I put out extra chairs.
LIZ. Well, let's us get a move on, then. Help me get this
potato salad on out there. I think I hear a car coming up

the lane now. God help us every one.

HALLIE. *[stops humming]* Hey, can I ask ...? Uh... What's a
News Bee?

LIZ. *[She keeps busy.]* A what, honey?

HALLIE. *[emphasizing each word]* A. <u>News. Bee</u>.

LIZ. I have no idea. *[to EMILY]* Ever hear of a ... what
was it, Hallie?

HALLIE. News Bee.

EMILY. Oh, News Bees. Well, I remember hearing old
folks talk about 'em. Aunt Pearl might be able to tell you
more than I could. Hand me that spoon, will you.

HALLIE. *[trying to keep EMILY on topic]* <u>News Bees</u>?

EMILY. A News Bee – uh – it would be a single, solitary
bee that came around to hang over somebody's head –
sort of hover and buzz. People used to think it brought
news of something happening ... or about to happen.

LIZ. Where's the tin foil?

EMILY. *[to LIZ]* Over by the sink. *[to HALLIE]* If it was a
yellow bee, it brought good news, they said. Said a black
bee brought bad news.

HALLIE. How did they know it was a News Bee and not
just some regular bee scouting around?

EMILY. Put that spoon with the potato salad, why don't
you. *[back to the News Bee]* Well, seems like they said if it
was indeed a News Bee, it would hang around over your
head and talk noise, then go on off ... heading straight for
a cemetery or some such place. That is, if it was a black
bee – <u>bad</u> news. In the old days, lots of people believed
in them. They usually paid attention when one came
around. *[in the moment]* Not there, Hallie. Set that bowl
over yonder.

HALLIE. *[pondering the News Bee news]* Okay.

EMILY. Where'd you hear about a News Bee, anyway?

HALLIE. I don't know. Somewhere. *[looking out kitchen
window]* Who's that?

EMILY. *[moves to screen door, looks hard into the distance]*
Oh, Lord, it's Aunt Pearl. And old Bert – hide the pies!
[They laugh] Will Ed's with 'em, that lanky youngster.

HALLIE. *[looking around sharply]* Will?

LIZ. *[oblivious to HALLIE's reaction, looking out the
window]* And here's Furman right behind, kicking up a

51

cloud on that old noisy bike of his. Lord, lord. Now they'll have to talk engines for a while, and you know those fellas — we'll never get 'em off that subject.

HALLIE. *[absently, recalling her dream]* It was a snake, wasn't it?

LIZ. What was, honey?

HALLIE. It was a snake. Snakebite. *[As HALLIE talks, she stares into space, as if seeing pictures that no one else can see.]* He was playing under the big sycamore down there by the river. His Aunt Tess was supposed to be watching him, but there was the clover chain they had started. She was trying to finish it ... for him to wear around his neck. He was tired of making it. Wandered off. The day ... it was sunny and bright, but they'd found some shade down there by the water.

LIZ. Who?

EMILY. What's this, now?

[LIZ & EMILY stop what they're doing and look at HALLIE.]

HALLIE. Clear as day. I saw it clear as day, and see it now.

LIZ. See what, Hallie?

HALLIE. That boy ... little Will. Our little cousin or uncle or somebody from way-back-when ... from the letter edged in black. He died of snakebite. She blamed herself for letting him get down under the washed-out roots of that big old tree growing out over the bank. The roots ... they were mostly exposed ... tangled. He was just a little thing. Crawled down in there to play when she wasn't watching. When he hollered, she went right to him, right away.

[LIZ and EMILY stare at HALLIE, looking from her to each other and back.]

HALLIE. She didn't know what had happened at first — why he was screaming. Didn't ever see the old snake. But when he started to swell, she found the two little puncture holes *[holds her left arm up at an angle above her head and points with two right-hand fingers to a specific spot on the underside of her left bicep]* — right here. Picked him up and ran hard as she could up here to the house.

LIZ. But how ...?

HALLIE. His mama tried everything she knew to do —

52

turned up the can of turpentine on the bite marks; cut and sucked and spit. But the poison had already spread into his bloodstream. They were here by themselves that day. By the time his Aunt Tess got him up here, it was too late ... already too late.

EMILY. Hallie ....

HALLIE. Don't ask me how I know. I don't know _how_ I know — I just know that I _know_. This is what happened. This is who they were. Tess and Annie and Little Will on the last day of his life. Right here. And how she made it through — his mama. And how his Auntie Tess suffered her guilt. [*She finally looks from EMILY to LIZ.*] He was a happy little boy. I know that. He was loved.

LIZ. But, Hallie, that had to be ...

EMILY. Had to be a hundred years ago, at least.

LIZ. Did you find a letter in that old box? Something that told that story?

HALLIE. No, ma'am. I don't know how I know this. Just that it's the truth. I feel it way down inside of me. I'm sure as I'm standing here that I'm telling you the truth ... but where that truth came from I do not know.

[*She looks into their faces, bewildered, as if searching for an answer. They have none.*]

EMILY. [*looking to LIZ*] I guess it must be Mamaw. She's here ... she's with us today.

HALLIE. Mamaw?

LIZ. How else could you know?

HALLIE. But ... you believe me?

LIZ. Of course we do, honey.

EMILY. Look at who you're talking to here. I still hear her voice on a regular basis, remember? You don't have to convince me.

LIZ. I think she's trying to convince herself, Em.

EMILY. Relax, Hallie. You've got good genes. Smart genes. Trust them. You don't have to know the _why_ of everything. You just need to trust what's in you.

HALLIE. [*still puzzled*] I see.

LIZ. Consider it luck. [*A beat.*] Now, girls, let's finish this up. We'll have two, three more hungry carloads coming in. Just pray that Lolly doesn't bring those damned, over-manicured, yip-yip dogs of hers. I don't think I could take them today, on top of everything else.

[LOLLY enters with a flourish. She feigns being indignant.]

LOLLY. Did I hear my name irreverently invoked? [then to HALLIE, humorously] Come give your decrepit Great-Aunt Lolly some sugar, Sugar! [calling through the screen door to unseen people outside/offstage] Y'all keep an eye on my pups out there. Don't let those fellas get too far from the house!

[She hugs HALLIE, gives quick greetings, and then is handed something to carry outside.]

LOLLY. Oh! Oka-ay.

[She takes the object, goes right back through the screen door to the porch, then looks offstage.]

LOLLY. Furman's arrived! Brother Boy, where in the hell have you been hiding? Get on up here, you!

LIZ. [reaching for courage with a deep breath, mentally preparing herself] Okay. Here it is. Here we go. [She picks up a foil-covered dish in each hand, exits backing through screen door, allowing it to bang shut behind her, then speaks from the porch] Uncle Furman! Please get your fuzzy face over here and take these baked beans off my hands!

[A man about 70 (FURMAN) steps onto the porch. He puts down his cooler and takes things from LIZ's hands, greeting her with a kiss on the cheek.]

EMILY. [to HALLIE] Good genes. Their memory is better than ours is sometimes.

HALLIE. [still confused and trying hard to sort it all out] I see. I do.

EMILY. [loads HALLIE's arms with a stack of paper plates, a stack of paper cups, the plastic utensils, and a jug of tea] Now, carry these outside, will you, honey? [opens the screen door with one hand and pushes HALLIE out with the other] We're gonna have us a mess of chicken-hungry folks pile in here in a whip-stitch.

[Left alone in the kitchen, EMILY continues to gather and prepare items to take outside, talking to herself.]

EMILY. My stars, Mamaw. My stars in heaven above.

[EMILY sticks a roll of paper towels under one arm, picks up a large platter covered in aluminum foil and exits, backing through the screen door, letting it slam after her.]

[*The sound of the arrival of another car is heard, perhaps with a honk tapping out a greeting.*]
EMILY. [*stepping over to the dinner bell and giving it a happy ring.*] Y'all come get it!
[*Lights fade on the empty kitchen.*]

SCENE 2

[*Outside* farmhouse, same day, *mid-afternoon*. *The* present.]

[*A picnic table laden with half-eaten food sits in the yard near back porch. The meal has been consumed, relatives relax around the picnic table and in yard chairs — EMILY, LOLLY (in her 60s or 70s), and FURMAN (70s). LIZ and HALLIE come and go. FURMAN rises and starts dumping trash into a garbage bag, beginning the clean-up.*]

[*All make small talk in familiar tones. They sit on the table benches and in folding lawn chairs, some of which are empty. Someone laughs at a memory that is being told.*]

[*A few other relatives are implied to be inside the house or wandering around the property, as indicated by occasional remarks and gestures toward these unseen people. Conversations overlap. A radio plays low in background.*]

LIZ. [*entering from the kitchen, quoting Mamaw*] "People, they's pie!"
[*All react in a way that shows that they recognize this announcement. Some chuckle; others are sentimental.*]
FURMAN. Lord have mercy, Lizzie. You sounded just like your Mamaw just then.
[*LIZ grins at him, gives him a peck on the cheek.*]
EMILY. [*calling to someone who is offstage*] Will Ed, honey, be careful in that old barn. [*to LOLLY*] The weeds are all grown up around it; looks like the roof could come down any second. [*calling to the unseen WILL ED offstage*] I'd hate to have to dig you out on a full stomach! [*to LOLLY*] It's just like a kid to want to go exploring. [*calling to the unseen boy again*] Why don't you at least take these dogs with you to scatter the snakes?
LOLLY. Oh, my lord, NO! My pups can't go into a mess

55

like that. [*She calls to dogs offstage.*] Algernon! Basil! SIT!
STAY! [*to EMILY*] Why, I never would get the beggar lice
and cuckleburrs out of them before I got them back home.
And they simply could NOT go into my house like that. Not
to mention the possibility of <u>snakebite</u>! [*to the unseen dogs,
whose yipping is heard offstage*] Boys, STAY!
FURMAN. [*indicating offstage toward the dogs*] You keep
those things inside your house, Lolly?
LOLLY. I most certainly do.
FURMAN. You don't sleep with 'em, do you?
LOLLY. [*chagrined*] Sometimes.
FURMAN. <u>What</u>? Naw!
LOLLY. Well, just if Algernon gets too lonesome. Or if
there's lightning. Basil can't abide lightning.
FURMAN. Well, I never. All right, then ... But you wouldn't
catch me with a damned <u>dog</u> in the <u>house</u>. Ever'body
knows <u>dogs</u> belong <u>outside</u> where they can hunt and run
around in God's creation. Still-and-all, I reckon it's whatever blows your skirt up, Lolly.
LIZ. Oh, now, Furman. Those aren't exactly some mangy
old rabbit hounds she's got. [*Changing the subject.*] Now,
where'd Pearl and Bert get to? I thought they were out
here.
EMILY. Last I saw 'em, they were in the front room —
reminiscing over the hearthstone.
LIZ. Seriously? I don't know why anybody'd get sentimental over an old coal grate.
EMILY. [*looks offstage in the direction of the river*] And I
think my baby brother'n'em took a little walk down to the
river. Been gone a while.
[*LIZ exits into the house.*]
LOLLY. [*sarcastically*] Well, thank you for your permission,
Furman. How I ever existed without it before now is a
mystery to me.
FURMAN. [*distracted*] No problem. [*He gestures toward
the gravel lane offstage.*] Who the hell's this, now?
LOLLY. [*looking in the same direction*] Must be somebody
that's lost. As Mamaw used to say: if you come back up
in here, you either know exactly where you're headed, or
else you're as lost as an Easter egg.
[*ALL look down the lane, trying to figure out who's driving*

56

toward them.]

LOLLY. Wait a minute.

FURMAN. Huh?

LOLLY. Wait just a pluperfect minute now.

EMILY. Who is it, Furman, can you tell? *[sudden recognition of who is approaching]* Unh-unh. Naw. Not today.

LOLLY. Please not today.

EMILY. This, we don't need.

FURMAN. *[with recognition]* Are you kiddin' me? Are you freakin' kiddin' me, now?

LOLLY. It isn't ...

FURMAN. Hell, yes, it is. It damned sure is, goddam it to all hell-and-back.

LOLLY. *[recognizing at last]* Well, I never. The nerve. The very nerve.

EMILY. Now, let's not lose our heads. Everybody stay as calm as possible. Let's just see how this plays out.

FURMAN. I can tell you exactly how this mess is about to play out. And you know it, too.

EMILY. We don't know anything as yet. Hold your water a minute. I'll get Liz out here.

[EMILY exits into the kitchen to find LIZ]

FURMAN. The very idea ....

LOLLY. Surely, it isn't ... oh! *[gets up, unnoticed by all, to cross in direction of unseen barking dogs' location]* Algie, Basil! Come, boys. Oh, my heart! Where've you gone now?

FURMAN. *[muttering to himself]* What kind of grief are you bringing this time, you no-good bastard? Come on, then. Sonofabitch. Bring it. Let's get this all said and done while we're still above ground.

EMILY. *[enters with LIZ; both stand on porch and look in direction of approaching car]* What's this about, do you think?

LIZ. I don't know, but it can't be good.

[The slam of a car door is heard offstage, and GARY, a man in his 70s, enters, chewing on a toothpick, looking suspiciously around the place, but avoiding the eyes of those who are watching him. Eventually, he speaks. He has obviously been drinking heavily.]

LOLLY. Gary? *[frustrated and at a loss]* Listen, I can't ... You can't ... We can't ... I mean, we just ...

GARY. What's all-a-this? Looks like y'all've seen a ghost. *[GARY feels his hip pocket, in which a small pistol is concealed; keeps his hand there for a moment]*

EMILY. *[in a cordial yet measured tone]* Hello, Uncle Gary.

GARY. *[to LIZ]* What, no greeting for your old man? No "welcome back, daddy dearest"?

LIZ. *[in a deferent but measured tone]* Dad.

GARY. What the hell's the matter with ever'body? Y'all acting kindly nervous. *[to FURMAN]* Somethin' on your mind, big brother?

FURMAN. What business've you got up in here, Gary?

GARY. Bid'ness? Why, <u>family</u> bid'ness, brother. Fam-i-ly <u>bid</u>'ness. I weren't expecting nobody to be 'round here. What're all a y'all doin' out here, anyhow, huh? Somebody die?

LOLLY. How dare you!

FURMAN. What's your angle this time?

GARY. *[laughs]* Angle? Always got to accuse me of having a angle or a evil plan of some kind or a — what do they call it? — a, yeah, a ulterior motive or somethin'. *[eyes narrow, tone changes]* Tell the truth now — you never have thought much of me, have you, Furman, you old sum'bitch?

FURMAN. What is it you want, Gary?

GARY. Always thought you were better than me, didn't you? Always lorded it over me, from the time we were kids. They let you get away with murder, just about. But not me. Not old Gary. Naw. I never got away with <u>shit</u>. *[He spits on the ground and glares at FURMAN.]*

FURMAN. What the hell nonsense're you talking this time?

GARY. Did I ever get what <u>I</u> wanted? Did anything ever swing <u>my</u> way in this outfit? <u>Hell</u>, no. Not a damned once't.

LOLLY. Jesus H. Christ on peanut butter toast, Gary! Not this again. You just never-ever learn, do you?!

FURMAN. Nobody's seen hide nor hair of you in years, Gary. Once they let you out of Eddyville, you just disappeared off the face of the earth, seemed like. We thought you were prob'ly dead by now.

GARY. <u>Hoped</u> I was dead is what you mean to say.

FURMAN. Whatever you think didn't go your way was your own damned fault. You made your bed.

GARY. I never even had a bed to make. I was outcast from

the start. 'Perfect Furman' set the pace and poor little Gary never could match it, so I just got left the hell out.

FURMAN. Screw you, Gary.

LOLLY. You need to turn around right this very minute and march yourself back to whatever hell you came from.

GARY. *[feels his hip pocket, keeps his hand there for a moment]* You never wanted to see me prosper, be liked, have what I wanted. *[He is nervous and his voice breaks.]* You never let me have the chance to prove what I could be. *[regains composure]* Well, *[sucks his teeth]* it don't make no difference now.

FURMAN. *[in a patronizing tone]* Pity poor Gary. Listen, boy, like I said before, you made your choices. Live with 'em. Don't you come whining 'round here. Not now. It's too late.

GARY. One thing I ain't is a whiner. And one thing I learned — it ain't <u>never</u> too late. And guess what, bro? I'm ba-a-ack. *[mocks FURMAN's patronizing tone]* 'Live with it.'

[GARY goes over to the edge of the porch, locates a certain loose board, indicates that it is right where he expected it, and pries the end up. He reaches under it and pulls out a dusty old liquor bottle.]

GARY. Good old Grandpoppa. *[Pulls out the cork and admires the bottle.]* He kept moving 'em around to hide 'em from me. But I knew all his little secret hidin' places. *[He takes a long swig and recorks the bottle.]*

LIZ. Dad, don't. Please don't come back like this. It's hard enough—everything is hard enough—without this.

GARY. *[still looking at FURMAN but speaking to LIZ]* And just whose side're you on, anyway, baby girl? *[turns to look at LIZ]* This is your old pap talking. Where's your loyalty, kid?

LIZ. I'm always on the side of family, Dad. The trouble is, we're <u>all</u> family here. We ought to all be on the <u>same</u> side.

LOLLY. For the love of pete. Will this dysfunctional mess never cease?

GARY. Well, I can see just what in the hell this is. This is a goddam ambush is what this is. By god if it ain't.

FURMAN. You the one came to us. We sure hadn't been

hidin' out waitin' for your sorry ass to show up. Now, I'm gonna ask you one more time — what is it that you want?

GARY. *[wheeling suddenly in a rage to face FURMAN]* I want MINE for a goddam change, that's what I want. I want what's mine, and this time, by god, I'm gonna get mine at the <u>head</u> of the line before you get yours. What do you think of that, Fur-Man?

FURMAN. And just what's left that you haven't already destroyed? What the hell do you think there is to get, Gary?

GARY. Well, hell ... *[indicating the property around them]* ... this. Whaddya think?

FURMAN. Are you telling me ... are you telling <u>us</u> that you have a notion that you ought to come waltzing in here and take over ever'thing that's left of this old place? Is that what you're saying? That it ought to all go to you and to hell with the rest of us? Who d'you think you are?

GARY. It's always been 'to hell with Gary' all these years. Now it's old Gary's time to say 'to <u>hell</u> ... <u>with</u> ... <u>YOU</u>.' I've come to get what's mine, and I aim to get it, whatever it takes. So, you can get with the program, or you can get the hell out of my way, boy.

FURMAN. You killed them off, and now you want to pick the bones, is that it?

LOLLY. You tell him, Furman!

GARY. You can shut the hell up now, Furman. You about to cross a line you don't want to cross.

LIZ. *[pleading]* Dad ... Dad!

FURMAN. To hell with your line. We've moved that line to accommodate you for years, you selfish bastard. I'm through with lines. I'll step any damned where I please.

EMILY. Uncle Furman ...

GARY. Then you'll step in a pile, brother. You'll step in a pile of shit so deep you'll never get the stink off your boots. *[dismissing him]* Now, get out of my way and let me talk to somebody that matters around here.

FURMAN. *[lunging toward GARY]* Why, you selfish sonofabitch! *[GARY steps backward in fear]* I'll kick your ass like I ought to've done years ago.

EMILY. *[stepping forward quickly to grab FURMAN]* Stop this now. It's not worth it. He's not worth it. Think of

60

Mamaw. <u>Think</u>, Furman!

[*FURMAN glares at GARY, hesitates, but gradually backs off.*]

GARY. What's a matter, Furry Man? No follow through? [*feels his hip pocket, keeps his hand there in anticipation*]

LIZ. [*in a placating tone*] Dad? You want some pie? Come on in and have you a piece of pie, why don't you? There's plenty.

GARY. Huh?

LIZ. Pie, Dad. You want a piece?

GARY. Pie? Hell, yes, I want a piece of the pie. What kind you got, little girl?

LIZ. All kinds. There's peach. Chocolate cream. Got some pecan left, I think. I'll go see.

[*LIZ exits into the kitchen*]

GARY. [*calling after her*] Pick me out something good, girlie. And don't make it no little sliver, neither. Pick me out one that's not yet been cut and bring it out here for me to see. I want whatever the rest of 'em hadn't bothered with. [*to FURMAN; leveling his voice into a growl*] I want the whole goddam thing.

FURMAN. [*dismissively and with disgust*] I gotta go.

EMILY. No, Uncle Furman. Please stay.

FURMAN. Nothing here for me anymore, I can see that. Thanks for the meal, hon. Y'all did real good with this old place. Y'all did right by it.

EMILY. We're <u>still here</u>, Furman. Just like always. And we need you with us.

[*FURMAN frowns, stares at her several seconds, shakes his head and relents, walks away from the group and warily watches GARY.*]

HALLIE. [*enters through the kitchen screen door*] Anybody seen my mom and dad? [*notices GARY*] Oh. Hi. [*looks more closely*] Uncle ... Gary?

GARY. That'd be me. And who might you be?

HALLIE. Uh, I'm, uh, Hallie.

LOLLY. Be careful, Hallie honey.

GARY. Hallie, huh? Hallie .... [*recognition*] My god. You little Hallie Linn? You Bill Ray's girl? All growed?

HALLIE. Yes, sir. [*she shudders, looks offstage as if into the distance*] Have ... have you seen my dad?

61

GARY. [*with abrupt suspicion*] He around here?

HALLIE. He was earlier. I'm just looking for him.

EMILY. Down to the river, honey. He and your momma went for a last walk.

HALLIE. I, uh …. [*senses trouble*] I need to look for them. I'm just gonna go … go find them.

[*HALLIE steps off porch and exits offstage.*]

GARY. [*in a suggestively vulgar manner*] Careful what you might come up on down there, girlie. No telling what kind of snakes're crawling about that riverbank this time of year. And some of the mean ones'll BITE. [*cackles bizarrely, looks toward the door*] Now, where's that nice pie I was clearly promised?

[*LIZ enters carrying a whole pie with meringue piled on top.*]

GARY. Ah, here she be. [*taking the pie from LIZ*] Give me that thang, baby girl. Look-at-here, Furry Man. The whole thing. <u>Mine</u> … to do with however I please. You prob'ly want a little piece, don't you?

FURMAN. I don't want a thing you got, Gary. But, so far, you got nothing. Just that cream pie there. And that ain't much … as per usual.

[*Overcome with a sudden burst of anger, GARY slams the pie, top down, on the porch floor in a rage — it splatters in every direction*]

LOLLY. Oh, my stars!

GARY. You smug sum'bitch! Here's what I got! [*Yanks a quarter-fold sheet of paper out of his shirt pocket and tosses it on the ground in FURMAN's general direction.*] Read it and weep, boy. Read it and weep.

EMILY. [*picks up the paper and unfolds it to read*] What's this?

LIZ. [*reads over EMILY's shoulder*] Dad, no! Why are you doing this? Can't we all just finish this up in peace?

GARY. Peace? I ain't had any peace in sebmty years. What's peace? This family never knew the meaning of the word.

FURMAN. Your mother did.

GARY. My mother never gave a shit about anybody but you.

LOLLY. [*indignant*] I beg your pardon!

GARY. Peace, hell. Mother made war against me all my goddamned life.

62

FURMAN. Cut the drama, Gary. It was the other way around and you damn well know it. You always brought the fight. There's victims ... but you sure as hell ain't one of 'em.

GARY. That little piece of paper there says I don't have to be pushed around by you no more, brother. I don't have to listen to you, I don't have to look at you, I don't have to have no dealings with you beyond settling this mess once't and for all. It was a sure-god power struggle, and it's lasted a long damned time ... but you lost, plain and simple, for I got the law with me! *[Feels for the pistol in his hip pocket, keeps his hand there for a moment.]*

FURMAN. What the hell is on this paper anyway? Give me that thing.

[EMILY hands it to him.]

GARY. What's on there is what I consider my birthright.

FURMAN. *[disgusted]* Name a god! *[reading]* Who is this lawyer, so-called? This Ned Sand? And what's this shit about a restraining order? *[Laughs at him.]* What the hell are you trying to come around and pull this time, Gary?

LOLLY. Same old horseshit, not much doubt about that.

GARY. I'm your worst nightmare, that's who in the hell I am. Knock, knock. *[singsong]* Guess who's ho-o-ome? *[indicates the house]* And I'm gonna enjoy living here. No mortgage, no brothers, no shit from no body. Yessir.

FURMAN. This idn't a legal document, Gary. Just a letter full a empty threats. Intimidation, that's all it is. Carries no weight. What. So. Ever. You can't come in here fakin' and bullyin' ever'body all over again and expect us to fall for that old line. Boy, you barkin' up the wrong tree this time. *[laughs at him]* You have no idea.

GARY. By god, that letter there says what I'm gonna do if you try to stop me from having what's mine. Grand-poppa told me when I was nothin' but *[voice breaks with emotion]* ... nothing but a little kid that this place'd be mine one of these days. Well, that day has by-god come. *[glares at the people and the table]* And I'm damn sure glad y'all're all here for it. Witness, Furman! Witness! *[gestures to himself]* Prodigal! *[cackles drunkenly]*

LIZ. But, Dad, it's all been said and done. It's already over.

GARY. Over? Hell, it's yet to begin. I'm here to claim my birthright, plain and simple, and that's what I aim to do. Whoever wants to stop me, step up right now.

LOLLY. Birthright?! What in the name of ...

EMILY. Uncle Gary, Great-Grandpoppa left this place to Mamaw, and in her will she left it to Liz and me.

GARY. The hell you say! Not a soul in this family ain't never had no will.

EMILY. Nawsir, it's true. It's all filed down at the courthouse. Has been for years. Nobody's lived here since Liz left it years ago, but we come out ever' so often ... keep the mowing done up. We just haven't had the heart to do anything about dispensing with the place until now.

GARY. [sidles drunkenly over to LIZ] Well, now, wait a minute, baby girl, now. Talk bid'ness with your old pap here. Don't you owe me something for bringing you into this mess you call family? How about looking out for me? Ain't I your family? Girl?

LIZ. You've always gotten your way pretty much, Dad, but it just won't work this time. It's out of our hands.

GARY. [wheedling] Not if you hold the deed. Come on, now. Let's talk this thing out ....

LIZ. Nothing to talk about. The road's comin' through here.

GARY. Huh?

LIZ. State took it. Took it all.

GARY. Now, what, now?

LIZ. We didn't have a choice in the matter. They confiscated ... or ... what's that word, Em?

EMILY. Condemned and appropriated the property.

GARY. They what? Who did?

LIZ. The government did. Highway department, I s'pose. D.O.T. Somebody.

LOLLY. That's pretty much the size of it.

GARY. They can't do that!

LOLLY. Bloomin' idiot.

FURMAN. They can and they did. Swallowed it up for that new four-lane they think they need.

GARY. The hell you say! But how? How do they get away with something like that — just condemning a man's property and taking it away?

FURMAN. Whose property?

GARY. [growls] Mine, goddam it.

LOLLY. Okay, that's it! We're done! Gary, you need to leave RIGHT NOW! Go on! Git!

FURMAN. They can do anything they damned well please. They're the gubment, ain't they? Same gubment that locked you up in the pen twice upon a long time ago. Should have thrown away the goddamned key while they had a chance.

GARY. They's only one key what matters. [pulls skeleton key out of his pocket and holds it aloft] And guess who's holding it?

LIZ. Dad. Listen to me. It's gone. All of it. Eminent domain. They paid us the minimum for it — they set the price. We used the money to pay property taxes, and we put the rest into a burial fund for any of us that might need it one of these days. Didn't amount to much. Wadn't enough to cut up and serve.

EMILY. We're putting the place to rest today. That's why we're all out here.

FURMAN. If you really were even a tiny part of this family, Gary — if you'd been around — you'd know that these girls have spent the last three, four days out here, cleaning up this place. They cleaned hell out of it, top to bottom. [with sentiment] They dressed it up, put Mother's old bedspreads on, made the whole place spic and span, what little's left in there.

EMILY. [quietly, reaching for LIZ's hand] Washing the body.

FURMAN. You'd of thought you were walking into it 20 years back; you'd of thought Mother was gonna come through that door to pitch out the wash water or carry a watermelon over there t'the table.

LOLLY. Lord love her sweet soul.

FURMAN. [smiles at EMILY and LIZ] Then these good, good women laid out a spread [indicates table] and called a gathering. And we heeded that call.

LIZ. We're here to say goodbye, Dad. It's a wake, sort of. We're out here to help Mamaw's place find its final rest. We wanted to give it a proper send off.

GARY. You all …. You …. [feels his hip pocket pistol again, keeps his hand there for a moment]

FURMAN. What's a matter, Gary? Got nuttin' to say now?

Here's your damned little phony letter. *[slaps it into GARY's chest]* You can't hold up this family no more, you freakin' bandit. There ain't n'more antique silver dollars in Mother's dresser drawer for you to filch; no more of Daddy's brand new equipment in the barn for you to steal and pawn. You cain't even sneak into the kitchen and take off with the biggest pork chop before supper. Your river's dried plumb up. You were a lucky little boy and could have been a lucky man, 'cause you had a family that loved you – a place to call home. Once was the time that you <u>had</u> the whole pie ... well, you squandered it. *[laughs at him]* I can see *[gestures at the pie mess on the porch floor]* it hadn't taught you a damned thing.

GARY. *[in helpless desperation]* But this <u>will</u> you spoke of .... Grandpoppa <u>TOLD</u> me ....

LOLLY. Told you what, exactly? Fool. Cur. Warty TOAD!

FURMAN. The only will you're in, Gary, is the one you haven't written for yourself yet. And the only thing you'll have to leave anybody is instructions – burial or cremation. You can go by dirt or you can go by fire, but, brother, you're gonna go just like the rest of us. We're all going. *[Looks up at the house and around the place.]* And some of us have already gone ... and won't never be back.

EMILY. We all just do the best we know how, Uncle Gary. The best we can do.

LIZ. Nobody's against you here, Dad.

GARY. But Grandpoppa said .... I was .... All this time I been .... *[Dissolves into silent, drunken sobs, stares at the key in his hand.]*

FURMAN. *[softens]* Let it go, Gary. It's over.

GARY. The hell it is! *[Drops the key; pulls small pistol out of his hip pocket and aims it at FURMAN]*

FURMAN. Whoa, now, Gary! Get a grip, boy!

LOLLY. Gary! No! Stop this NOW!

GARY. I <u>got</u> a grip ... *[shakes pistol]* ... on the only thing'll do me any good. 'Boy.' See you in Hades.

[GARY aims drunkenly at FURMAN and squeezes the trigger. FURMAN winces, throwing his hands in front of his face. The gun clicks and misfires. It is not loaded.]

GARY. Goddammit! *[looks at the gun, clicks it again, flings it to the ground]* Sonofabitch!

66

LOLLY. Oh, my heart!

GARY. Won't I ever get no peace in this hateful world? Cain't I ever do one goddam thing right? All I ever wanted .... All I ever ....

[GARY dissolves again into drunken sobs. The others stare at him in shock. After a moment, LIZ bends down to pick up the key. She places it into her pocket and moves gently toward him.]

LIZ. It's all right, Daddy. Come on in the kitchen with me. Come let's see what's left of this dinner. We'll get you fed, get you some coffee.

[LIZ looks apologetically at EMILY and FURMAN, leads the staggering GARY by his elbow; they exit the porch and enter the house.]

LOLLY. Goddess bless us, every one. [Spent, she collapses into a chair, fanning herself.]

EMILY. You all right, Uncle Furman?

FURMAN. I'll make it. [picks up pistol; is still shaken but tries to collect himself] Why, the very idea .... Come in here with a flimsy-assed piece of paper telling people what's what. And pulling a goddam gun! He's been that way since he was the runt of the litter. What in the name of God is he thinking, trying to pull a stunt like that? Actin' like he's the one needs protection from us!

EMILY. [shaken] Oh, my God. I thought I'd lost you, too.

FURMAN. I'm okay, honey. I'll be okay in a minute. It's finally over. It's done with.

EMILY. We have got to try to let this go. All of it. We're all bruised. But Gary's honest-to-god broken.

FURMAN. The day has come, and it has passed.

EMILY. [after a beat or two, collecting herself] I miss Mom and Daddy the most when I'm with you, you know that? Don't tell, but you always were my favorite, Uncle.

FURMAN. I see my sister in your face, girl. I miss her every day ... and that ornery old daddy of yours, too. But you're the best one of us, honey. You and Lizzie Bit have made us all think twice. About who we are, who we were. Maybe even about who we want to be. [They hug; then he holds her at arms length and looks into her eyes] I do thank ye for that.

[EMILY wipes her eyes and smiles; punches him playfully]

EMILY. Don't go gettin' all weepy on me, Furman. You'll make me ruin my complimentary Merle Norman treatment.

FURMAN. What you talking about, Em? You're as fair of face as the day is long. Don't you ever start going Merle Norman on me. [*puts his arm around her, comfortingly*] Y'take after your good-looking uncle here, don't you? [*They share a smile.*]

EMILY. Have we really done right by this old place, Furman? Should we have fought harder or paid more attention to it these past few years? Would it've changed anything?

FURMAN. Time and events are bound to flow, just like that river out yonder. You said it yourself, honey: we all do the best we can; best we know how. You and Lizzie have done that. You and this old place can rest.

EMILY. Have we done right by Liz's daddy, though? He's blood, you know.

FURMAN. All I know is that both the living and the dead have done what we can for Gary, and nothin' seems to work. In the end, nobody's responsible for a grown man but himself. He'll have to find his own peace however he can.

EMILY. I just feel so sorry for Liz. And sometimes for him, too, I guess. You saw him — ranting and raving one minute, crying like a baby the next.

FURMAN. He's looking right pitiful, idn't he? He can really play it. And I truly am sorry for him, but I'm damned if I trust him. Never could. Well, you saw what just happened. I grew up with that. I watched your Mamaw live scared to death of him. He's like a snake you run over in the road. Your tires roll it over and it's just stunned for a minute, but before long it comes to and shimmies off toward more mischief.

EMILY. You reckon he'll ever find what he's searching for?

FURMAN. I doubt it. Well, I can't say. But I do hope he does, for Liz's sake. I don't know where he got that sour, hateful outlook. There might be somebody out there that can find what little good's left in him ... if there is any. They say nobody's ever all bad, but I don't know. Gary's just stayed confused his whole life. Comes out in meanness.

EMILY. Why do you think that is?

FURMAN. Haven't the foggiest notion. You?

EMILY. Nope. I hate it for him, though. It's pretty much over for us, now that this place is gone. I don't expect I'll see him again. But I reckon he'll still be out there ...
searching.

FURMAN. Yep. I won't miss him much, though. That's sad but true. It's all one sad, sorry mess.

EMILY. [after a beat, attempting to straighten herself up and get busy again] Well, I don't know where everybody's gotten off to.

[EMILY grins and points to LOLLY in the chair, arm thrown across her eyes. FURMAN shakes his head knowingly, smiles and shrugs.]

EMILY. Anyway, I've gotta go in and start packin' up.

FURMAN. Can you use a hand?

EMILY. Always.

[They cross to the table and start gathering food containers, trash, etc., and carry them inside the kitchen.]
[LOLLY remains collapsed in her chair, oblivious.]
[Lights fade.]

SCENE 3

[Scene is _outside_ same farmhouse, same day, now _early evening, still daylight_. _The present._ LIZ is sitting on empty back porch steps. There is a stack of folded quilts, bedspreads and a cooler beside her. EMILY comes out, covered pie tin in one hand, basket in the other. She sets down the basket and pie.]

LIZ. You said it was coming. I just didn't want to believe it. But seems like Time has a mind of its own.

EMILY. It does. So. Here it is.

LIZ. Here it is.

EMILY. [looking at the house] Well, the place is clean as a whistle now, anyway. It's ready to cross over.

LIZ. Mmm-hmm.

EMILY. And 'most ever'body got whatever little possessions they wanted ... and then some.

LIZ. Nobody came to actual blows. Bad as it was, it was nearly a whole lot worse.

69

EMILY. I was relieved.

LIZ. Mamaw must be relieved. [*She speaks to the air around them.*] Well, how about it, Mamaw? How'd we all do?

EMILY. Aunt Pearl's the oldest left among us, so she'd be the one to know. Before she and old Bert left, Pearl proclaimed that we sure enough did Mamaw proud.

LIZ. I hope to goodness we did.

EMILY. [*indicating offstage, implying their parked cars*] Say, unless my eyes deceive me, I saw you loading up a box with model train track sticking out of it.

LIZ. Could you believe it? After all my worrying about that old thing, and then Roy didn't even show up. Well, that's one more box I'll stick up in my own attic and give it to him next time I see him, I reckon.

EMILY. Broken smokestack and all, I s'pose. [*She hesitates.*] You coming back out here tomorrow?

LIZ. I think I want to. I think I can now. [*She notices EMILY looking at her with surprise.*] I know. I'm surprised at myself. But I'd like to see this through, now I've started it.

EMILY. I don't think I can take it.

LIZ. I'm glad we talked the road crew out of using the dozer.

EMILY. Seemed too ... I don't know ... violent, maybe. Unbecoming the dignity of the place.

LIZ. Yeah, cremation seems fitting. It seems right.

EMILY. Still, I know I couldn't set the torch.

[*HALLIE enters from house.*]

HALLIE. I'm heading out.

EMILY. Hallie, honey, you're one of a kind.

LIZ. [*grinning*] Or one of a very small group, anyway.

HALLIE. I hate to admit it — I mean, I <u>REALLY</u> hate to admit it — but if it weren't for you two, a piece of me'd be missing in action. So, thanks.

[*LIZ holds up the skeleton key*]

LIZ. Now, girls, here's the key to this old homeplace. What should we do with it?

EMILY. I don't know. Won't be needed anymore.

HALLIE. Right. Aunt Lolly said she wants the door.

EMILY. She what?!

HALLIE. That's what she said. Said she's going to use it

70

for one of her art projects.

[*EMILY & LIZ express looks of skepticism and confusion.*]

HALLIE. [*shrugs*] Who knows — it's Lolly, right? Said she's sending somebody out here to pick it up early-early tomorrow morning ... before ....

EMILY. Well, if that doesn't beat all.

LIZ. I was thinking I'd give this key to you, Hallie.

HALLIE. [*pleased*] Yeah?

LIZ. Yeah. But then I got to thinking, what in the world would Hallie want with an old skeleton key?

EMILY. Oh, I've a feeling she'll think of something.

LIZ. It's yours then.

[*LIZ hands HALLIE the key.*]

EMILY. That seems right.

[*HALLIE's face clouds when she takes the key.*]

LIZ. [*to HALLIE*] Honey, what's troubling you?

HALLIE. I'm not exactly sure. But when I took hold of this key ...

EMILY. Should we worry now or worry later?

HALLIE. It's probably nothing. Whatever it is, it feels like it's meant to be for the best. Maybe. Anyhow ... thanks, Liz. This ... this is going right into my treasure box.

[*HALLIE hugs LIZ.*]

HALLIE. Well, I better get going.

LIZ. You take care of yourself, hon.

[*HALLIE hugs EMILY.*]

EMILY. Call if you need to.

[*HALLIE exits. Her car is heard driving away.*]

LIZ. You think it's the sight? You think there's still more to bear?

EMILY. It's life, Liz. Never ending. What comes'll come ... because it has to. One thing I do know is that our little Hallie tried to do the sitting up last night. Tried to see the old house through its last full moon. Out of respect.

LIZ. Wonder if she made it 'thout fallin' asleep?

EMILY. I don't know.

LIZ. Well, it was good of her to try.

EMILY. She's a good girl. [*a beat*] Your daddy all right?

LIZ. He'll be fine. For him.

EMILY. Y'all get things straightened out between you?

LIZ. We talked a long time, and it was good. We made

71

our peace. I reckon he accepts that he's got nothin' left here, and I finally accept that, too. When you feel like you've got nothin', then you've got nothin' to lose. That might explain him ... a little. Anyway, he seemed different somehow — like he was kind of gettin' ready for ... whatever's next. Ready to move on. Didn't even seem that torn up about it, to tell you the truth.

EMILY. Well, that's something anyway. When will you see him next?

LIZ. He's gone for good, I expect. You know him ... always got the next move planned, knows where he's gonna run to. Doesn't look back. Said he reckoned he might head downriver to Memphis. Not much telling with him just <u>what</u> he'll do.

EMILY. You're not still feeling guilty, are you?

LIZ. Oh, there's probably still some guilt deep down. I don't expect I've felt the last of it. But, no, I b'lieve I can pretty much let go now. Of this. Of him. Of the life I wished for ... and the disappointment long held by that lonesome little girl who lives inside me. She's getting pretty good at adjusting.

EMILY. Had plenty of practice, hasn't she, hon? That little girl inside. Don't lose her completely, though. She's still part of you. A really good part.

LIZ. I'll try to remember to tell her that when she starts giving me trouble.

[A beat as they ponder the inevitable.]

EMILY. It'll be a long time before I can even drive out this way, I bet.

[Another thought-filled beat.]

EMILY. Well ... no silver coins, but we got through it for this old place, so maybe we can get through it for one another some distant day.

LIZ. In a manner of speaking. [Another beat, leading to a sort of acceptance.] Well, I reckon I'm fixin' to go on home, too. Gotta be back out here early tomorrow.

EMILY. Purge and purify.

LIZ. You sure you won't meet me out here in the morning?

EMILY. I think I just can't stand any more of this. After all that drama today, I think I'm done.

LIZ. Well. I now know that I can stand a whole lot more than I think. We all can ... if we have to. [a beat] All right

72

then, if I don't go now, I never will. And how could that possibly come to any good end? [*hugs her cousin goodbye.*] Bye, Emmers. And thanks for ....

EMILY. Goodbye, Lizzabutt. Come see me 'fore long, y'hear?

LIZ. [*She piles quilts on cooler, picks it up and crosses, not looking back.*] I hear.

[*LIZ exits across the yard. The sound of a car door, followed by an engine starting and then receding into the distance. EMILY stands watching; she blows LIZ a kiss and waves her arm above her head, just as ANNIE had done in the first flashback scene.*]

[*EMILY looks around the porch one last time, taking it all in. She peers through the window; picks up the basket.*]

EMILY. OK, Mamaw, how about you just come on up home with me now — hmm? [*Then, in a tempting, sing-song tone ...*] I've got a gracious plenty of <u>pie</u>.

[*EMILY exits across the yard. Her car is heard driving away.*] [*Lights down.*]

SCENE 4

[<u>Night</u>. <u>The present</u>. *Same day. GARY enters on foot. He is drunk, and he staggers. In one hand he carries a bottle of liquor. He also carries his bedroll or backpack. He crosses a little downstage of the house and stops.*]

GARY. I've been made to wait long enough. <u>Long</u>. <u>E</u>. <u>Nuff</u>! [*Music rises as GARY walks around surveying the house, the distant river, the land, the garden. He crosses to the porch, drops his backpack/bedroll and sits. He talks to himself drunkenly and in self-piteous surrender.*]

GARY. Man ain't got no home, man ain't got no peace. No purpose. [*He takes a swig.*] My insides is all bloody scabs. Only one way to heal 'em up. Only one <u>right</u> way.

GARY. [*takes another swig.*] I'm so damned tired. Got to rest. Got to! Some-damn-how. Lookin' for the handle ... get a <u>grip</u> on this life.

[Drinks last of bottle and tosses it aside. Grabs backpack/ bedroll and stands.]

[Music and lights shift to indicate GARY's inner darkness.]

GARY. Man with any pride's got to be in charge of his <u>own</u> destiny.

[He crosses to door, opens it and tosses in the backpack/bed-roll. Then he turns and crosses toward side of house.]

GARY. Y'all shoulda known that this ain't never gonna be over 'til <u>I</u> say it's over. And I say <u>NOW</u>!

[He pulls out a gas can from under the edge of the porch and, while crossing, unscrews it. He opens the door. He backs into the house, pouring the gas into the kitchen area. He tosses the can aside, reaches into his pocket, and takes out a Zippo lighter. He lights it.]

GARY. I'll be there <u>first</u> this time, Mother!!

[Music cuts out. There is a silent beat as he holds up the lighter, then as if in surprised recognition...]

GARY. Grandpoppa?!?

[He drops the flame. There is an explosion of light and the sound of a fiery whoosh. <u>Blackout</u>. The dinner bell clangs once. Silence.]

EPILOGUE

[During blackout, all characters take places, facing upstage, except 'FUTURE HALLIE' who faces the audience. All begin softly <u>humming</u> the hymn 'FARTHER ALONG.']

[FUTURE HALLIE, in her top-of-show light downstage right, stands wearing the precious <u>skeleton key</u> prominently as a necklace.]

[Each character will turn downstage before speaking their in-dividual lines. Other characters continue <u>humming</u> the hymn at low volume throughout the dialogue.]

TESS. How does one overcome regret and sorrow?
HALLIE. Time.
ANNIE. What helps us cope when Nature turns against us?
HALLIE. Courage.
LIZ. What makes the wounds of betrayal finally heal?
HALLIE. Distance.
EMILY. How can we accept things we do not understand?
HALLIE. Trust. But ... what shapes us, underneath it all?

[*The remaining characters turn downstage.*]

ALL [*except HALLIE*]. Home.

[*ALL <u>sing</u> with joy the hymn 'FARTHER ALONG.' *]
[*traditional; new lyrics by Stephen Reinhardt]*

Tempted and tried, we're oft made to wonder
Why it should be thus, not knowing why.
But we shall cling to hope everlasting.
We'll understand it all by and by.

Farther along we'll know all about it.
Farther along it all will be shown.
Brothers and sisters, live in the sunshine.
We'll understand it, goin' up home.

We'll understand it, goin' up home.
Yes, we'll understand it, goin' up home.

~ CURTAIN ~

Gallery

Images from the 2022 premiere of
"Goin' Up Home"

79

ABOUT THE PLAYWRIGHT

SCOUT LARKEN LINK lives & writes in a hermitage
tucked into a cedar & hardwoods grove
at the end of the road in rural central Kentucky.

Among Scout's many published writings is
SLANT, a novel set in rural Kentucky.